THE CHRISTIAN
AS A
CONSUMER

POTENTIALS
GUIDES FOR PRODUCTIVE LIVING

Wayne E. Oates, General Editor

THE CHRISTIAN AS A CONSUMER

by

DENISE GEORGE

THE WESTMINSTER PRESS
Philadelphia

Scripture quotations from the Revised Standard Version of the Bible are copyrighted 1946, 1952, © 1971, 1973 by the Division of Christian Education of the National Council of the Churches of Christ in the U.S.A., and are used by permission.

Book Design by Alice Derr

First edition

Published by The Westminster Press ®
Philadelphia, Pennsylvania

PRINTED IN THE UNITED STATES OF AMERICA
9 8 7 6 5 4 3 2 1

Library of Congress Cataloging in Publication Data

George, Denise.
  The Christian as a consumer.

  (Potentials)
  Bibliography: p.
  1. Simplicity—Religious aspects—Christianity.
  2. Economics—Religious aspects—Christianity.
  I. Title. II. Series.
  BV4647.S48G46 1984   241'.64   83-26062
  ISBN 0-664-24518-8 (pbk.)

For
Dr. and Mrs. John W. Hughston

friends so dear
they have become family

Contents

Foreword

The eleven books in this series, Potentials: Guides for Productive Living, speak to your condition and mine in the life we have to live today. The books are designed to ferret out the potentials you have with which to rise above rampant social and psychological problems faced by large numbers of individuals and groups. The purpose of rising above the problems is portrayed as far more than merely your own survival, merely coping, and merely "succeeding" while others fail. These books with one voice encourage you to save your own life by living with commitment to Jesus Christ, and to be a creative servant of the common good as well as your own good.

In this sense, the books are handbooks of ministry with a new emphasis: coupling your own well-being with the well-being of your neighbor. You use the tools of comfort wherewith God comforts you to be a source of strength to those around you. A conscious effort has been made by each author to keep these two dimensions of the second great commandment of our Lord Jesus Christ in harmony with each other.

The two great commandments are given in Luke 10:25–28: "And behold, a lawyer stood up to put him to the test, saying,

'Teacher, what shall I do to inherit eternal life?' He said to him, 'What is written in the law? How do you read?' And he answered, 'You shall love the Lord your God with all your heart, and with all your soul, and with all your strength, and with all your mind; and your neighbor as yourself.' And he said to him, 'You have answered right; do this, and you will live.' "

Underneath the two dimensions of neighbor and self there is also a persistent theme: The only way you can receive such harmony of thought and action is by the intentional re-centering of your life on the sovereignty of God and the rapid rejection of all idols that would enslave you. The theme, then, of this series of books is that these words of Jesus are the master guides both to the realization of your own potentials and to productive living in the nitty-gritty of your day's work.

The books in this series are unique, and each claims your attention separately in several ways.

First, these books address great social issues of our day, but they do so in terms of your own personal involvement in and responses to the problems. For example, the general problem of the public school system, the waste in American consumer-ism, the health hazards in a lack of rest and vocational burnout, the crippling effects of a defective mental outlook, and the incursion of Eastern mystical traditions into Western Christian activism are all larger-than-life issues. Yet each author translates the problem into the terms of day-to-day living and gives concrete guidelines as to what you can do about the problem.

Second, these books address the undercurrent of helpless-ness that overwhelming epidemic problems produce in you. The authors visualize you throwing up your hands and saying: "There is nothing *anyone* can do about it." Then they show you that this is not so, and that there are things *you* can do about it.

Third, the authors have all disciplined themselves to stay off their own soapboxes and to limit oratory about how awful the world is. They refuse to stop at gloomy diagnoses of incurable conditions. They go on to deal with your potentials for changing yourself and your world in very specific ways. They do not let you, the reader, off the hook with vague, global utterances and generalized sermons. They energize you with a sense of hope that is generated by basic information, clear decision-making, and new directions taken by you yourself.

Fourth, these books get their basic interpretations and recommendations from a careful plumbing of the depths of the power of faith in God through Jesus Christ. They are not books that leave you with the illusion that you can lift yourself and your world by pulling hard at your own bootstraps. They energize and inspire you through the hope and strength that God in Christ is making available to you through the wisdom of the Bible and the presence of the living Christ in your life. Not even this, though, is presented in a namby-pamby or trite way. You will be surprised with joy at the freshness of the applications of biblical truths which you have looked at so often that you no longer notice their meaning. You will do many "double takes" with reference to your Bible as you read these books. You will find that the Bread of Life is not too holy or too good for human nature's daily food.

You need only to look at your monthly bills to see that the prophet Haggai was right: "He who earns wages earns wages to put them into a bag with holes" (Hag. 1:6b). You are blessed indeed today if you have an opportunity to earn wages, because unemployment seems to be a devilish side effect of reducing inflation, shifts from national to international markets, expanding population due to unrestrained reproduction, refugee resettlement, and the aging of both industrial equipment and the people who know only how to use that equipment.

Denise George, a theologically educated young matron, the mother of two children, and a writer with two books already published, addresses you and me as Christians who not only earn money but spend it. We are Christian consumers. Therefore, her consistent and primary emphasis is upon the ways our Christian beliefs shape or do not shape our *behaviors* in the use of money. She develops the themes of our calling and our consecration as Christians to value persons above things, to worship God rather than the opinions of those around us about what we buy, own, or conspicuously try to afford. She shows how simplifying our desires and lifestyles can bring more genuine contentment and how skillful management can set free more of our money for the more lasting things of life such as good memories, better educations, and better health. She assesses the hazards of the plastic credit card, the use of junk foods vs. basic home-prepared foods, and the insistence upon our always buying the newest and latest of everything.

However, the motive the author gives for being a canny and wise Christian consumer is not a desire to hoard and become miserly. On the contrary, we save so that we can *share* with the hungry, naked, and cold ones for whom Christ died. She concludes her book with a remarkable appeal to Americans, who are such a small percentage of the population of the world and who consume such a large percentage of the goods of the world, to *share* our abundance of goods with the poor and starving people of the world. Furthermore, we are to do this on an emergency basis at the same time that we share our know-how and technology to increase the production of food and clothing by the underdeveloped nations of the earth.

WAYNE E. OATES

Louisville, Kentucky

Acknowledgments

I am grateful, indeed, to Dr. Wayne E. Oates for his kind pastoral direction in the writing of this book, for his support and encouragement on this project as well as on others, and for his constant inspiration. I count it a great honor to know him.

To Dr. Roger Omanson, my professor of New Testament at Southern Baptist Theological Seminary, for his help with and suggestions for this book, for his many classes of valuable instruction, and for his friendship, I am deeply indebted.

And to my husband, Dr. Timothy George, who supports me in everything I undertake, who helps transport library books back and forth, who listens patiently to hours of endless ideas, who offers me much-appreciated professorial advice, and who goes far beyond the role of "daddy" in caring for our toddler son, Christian, so that I can write, my heartfelt thanks and everlasting devotion.

Chapter 1

Money—
A Necessary Evil?

You and I, along with most people in our society, deal with money on two levels. Right at the top of our attention is our struggle to get money and our impulse to spend or not to spend the money we get. But deep down beneath, down in the bottom of our hearts, are some attitudes, basic beliefs, and convictions (if you will permit me to say so) that shape and determine both how we get money and how we spend it. My plan is to deal first with these attitudes, beliefs, and convictions in the light of Jesus Christ's teachings. The searchlight of his loving understanding will help us to get at what makes us do as we do with money, and to change that if need be. Then I will pinpoint specific things we can do to bring our actions into line with a reexamined heart, newly chosen attitudes, reshaped beliefs, and convictions brightly lighted with the presence of Christ.

Let me begin with a familiar story.

As a child I delighted in hearing the story of Cinderella. No doubt you, too, know it by heart. A poor young woman was cruelly treated by her stepmother and stepsisters. While they attended the festive king's ball, Cinderella remained home to scrub the floors, unaware that later that very evening she would be approached by a magical fairy godmother. She would be changed instantly from rags to riches and go elegantly gowned to the extravaganza. Before the clock struck midnight, through a glass shoe entanglement, Cinderella would become the most sought after young woman in the kingdom. At the end of the story, Cinderella becomes the wife of the handsome prince. And she would live out her life "happily ever after."

The American Success Story—In Reverse

Would you enjoy the drama as much if Cinderella had been the wife of the rich prince at the beginning of the story, and through a series of events, ended up as a poor little girl in rags? I wouldn't. Would it make a difference to you if Cinderella had chosen voluntarily to step off the royal consumer merry-go-round, perhaps finding her riches in things not related to crystal shoes and fine coaches? The story would not hold the same excitement and fascination for me, even if Cinderella had chosen a simpler life-style, perhaps a kind of voluntary poverty. You will probably agree that the "American success story" suited Cinderella well.

From Riches to Rags

Jesus' life was somewhat like a Cinderella story in reverse. Paul explained to the Corinthians: "You know the grace of our Lord Jesus Christ, that though he was rich, yet for your sake he became poor, so that by his poverty you might become rich" (II Cor. 8:9). Indeed, for your sake and for my sake Jesus left his royal robes behind him. He took the form of a baby born to poor, hardworking parents. His lot was voluntary poverty. To be sure, Jesus lived a life nurturing and identifying with the poor. In the Gospel of Matthew, Jesus admits: "Foxes have holes, and birds of the air have nests; but the Son of man has nowhere to lay his head" (Matt. 8:20). Jesus also asked of those who would follow him the same. He sent out his twelve companions to preach and to heal with clear advice about their possessions: "Take nothing for your journey, no staff, nor bag, nor bread, nor money; and do not have two tunics" (Luke 9:3).

As you read of Jesus' ministry, you may have discovered that Jesus continually encouraged others who were seeking the kingdom of God to trade their earthly possessions for eternal riches. Of some, like chief tax collector Zacchaeus, Jesus did not demand the selling and distribution of all possessions. Upon their meeting, Zacchaeus only promised: "Lord, the *half* of my goods I give to the poor; and if I have defrauded any one of anything, I restore it fourfold" (Luke 19:8). To which Jesus replied: "Today salvation has come to this house" (Luke 19:9). But for others, such as his twelve disciples, Jesus' words "Follow me" meant leaving everything they owned—nets, boats, businesses, and marketplace profits.

In some cases, the call of Jesus to discipleship and the offer of salvation depended solely on how people decided to handle their financial affairs. This point is powerfully illustrated in the story of the rich young ruler (Luke 18:18–24; cf. Mark 10:17–22). You've probably read the story many times.

A rich young man knelt before Jesus with an urgent question: "Good Teacher, what shall I do to inherit eternal life?" Jesus looked into the eyes of this sincere young man and loved him. Then Jesus offered him wealth far more abundant than the world could ever offer. But with that same loving spirit Jesus added: "One thing you still lack. Sell all that you have and distribute to the poor, and you will have treasure in heaven; and come, follow me." As you know, the story ends on a sad note. The young man could not part with his possessions. He enjoyed the security he thought only money could bring. No doubt, as Jesus spoke to him of becoming voluntarily poor, he had the same visions you and I might have. He could envision old age with no financial security, a life spent begging with the city's poorest beggars. The thought of the Cinderella story in reverse made him fear for his present and his future.

Can you sense the regret of this young man as he turned and walked away from Jesus? He would, perhaps, have an entire lifetime to hear the echo of Jesus' words and to reflect on his decision.

How do you understand the story of the rich young ruler? I must confess to you that Jesus' command leaves me wondering what I should do about my possessions. As a Christian, should I sell all that I own? Should I drain my checking account and distribute the small balance to the poor? How could I buy groceries and clothes, or meet my mortgage payments? How could I pay for my children's education, buy medical and life insurance, and plan for my retirement? If you sold everything you had and gave it all away, how would you eat? Where would you sleep? How could you provide for your family's needs? As you and I apply the situation to our own lives, perhaps the answer the rich young ruler gave to Jesus does not seem so wrong. This young man probably worried about the same problems you and I struggle with today.

How do you interpret Jesus' words to the rich young ruler? Perhaps you have long pondered their meaning. Could Jesus look into the young man's heart and see an overwhelming love for money, a love so consuming that it had no room for Jesus? Perhaps if you and I could just put our bank accounts in their proper place—second to God—then we could keep our bank accounts open and enjoy what we have. But how do you read Jesus' statement after his offer of salvation was turned down? "How hard it is for those who have riches to enter the kingdom of God! For it is easier for a camel to go through the eye of a needle than for a rich man to enter the kingdom of God" (Luke 18:24–25). Did Jesus believe that money itself was evil?

Doris Donnelly writes: "The Christian gospel . . . tells us that money itself is not the issue; the real issue is how we get it and what we do with it. . . . Money may not be intrinsically evil, but in its comings and goings in our lives it is frequently the root of evil." (Doris Donnelly, "The Needle's Eye: Christians and Their Money," *The Christian Century,* April 27, 1983, p. 400.) Do you agree with her?

What Did Jesus Mean?

You may believe, as others do, that the rich cannot be saved. Perhaps they are already in possession of their rewards and thus cannot take part in God's plan of redemption. You may think this to be especially true if the riches were achieved at the expense of others.

Or maybe you agree with Hugh Martin when he writes: "If riches stand in the way of the higher interests of life, material comfort and well-being must be sacrificed. When Jesus asked rich people to give up their wealth he was urging a moral choice, not laying down a universal law. Only in one case is the surrender of everything made a condition of discipleship, and that was probably an exceptional case demanding exceptional treatment." (Hugh Martin, *Christ and Money,* p. 33.)

Perhaps you believe, along with some Christians, that Jesus only recommended that the rich young ruler give away his possessions, but that it need not be done in order to achieve salvation. Through disposal of material things, the young man could have just become more perfect in God's eyes.

Jacques Leclercq states that attitude was responsible for Jesus' request. "Jesus asks the young man to give up his possessions, and the young man refuses; the reason can only be that he clings to them. . . . A Christian should cling to nothing, but be ready to give up everything for the sake of the Kingdom." (Jacques Leclercq, *Christianity and Money*, p. 27.)

Again I ask, how do you understand the meaning of Jesus' words? Do you believe that your salvation rests on your decision about what you do with your money? Needless to say, the issue is a confusing one. As I study the text and read the opinions of others, I always come back to face the same questions posed by Luke T. Johnson in his book *Sharing Possessions: Mandate and Symbol of Faith* (pp. 15–16): "If I am rich, am I automatically excluded from God's care? . . . Is wealth determined by the quantity of material things I have or the degree of my attachment to them? Or is there something evil about possessions as such which taints everyone to some degree, and more when more is owned? . . . Must I divest myself of all I own and become destitute or only become uncomfortable?"

I must also ask: Just what did Jesus mean by "riches"? How much money makes one rich? Perhaps the rich young ruler was considered rich by his counterparts because he could afford to eat three square meals a day, had an indoor Roman-style bathroom, and possessed a change of clothes. In the United States, the very poor may own a house and a car, eat well, and send their children to good public schools. A poor family living in the streets in Bangladesh may consider the most impoverished United States citizen to be wealthy in comparison. How many material objects in your home or how much cash in your savings account makes you rich? How do Jesus' words to the rich young ruler apply to your life and my life as Christians of today? And, most important, how can we gain further understanding as to the meaning or meanings of Jesus' words?

As no absolute authority on the Bible exists, you and I can only gain needed insight through prayer and study. As you read and listen to the opinions of others, you must always depend on the Holy Spirit to speak to your own heart. Be open to him, live as a learner, and direct your life as he speaks to you.

Are You Called to the Simple Life?

Has Jesus called you to a simple life? He calls some to take a vow of poverty, like the priest, monk, and nun. Others, like Zacchaeus, he asks to part with only a portion of their possessions, living a far simpler life-style, and giving more money to the poor. Jesus often directs his disciples into different areas of ministry. Some receive the call to foreign mission service in primitive and remote villages. There they must drastically change their style of living to identify with the native people. Others feel led to work in inner-city situations. They move into deteriorating, cramped apartments and try to adapt to the life-style of the tenants to whom they minister. Some Christians feel called to live in Christian communities. They simplify their needs, give up private possessions, and share together a life of commitment to God. Jesus does, indeed, call his followers into varying areas of service. You may have already answered his call to a simple existence. If so, you know for yourself what Jesus' words mean. Perhaps you have given up those things dear to you, whether family, friends, possessions, or money. To you, following Jesus means a life of sacrifice and service. And you may often wonder, as I do, about people in Christian service who give up little to follow Christ. I'm sure you know people who have become Christians and who haven't given up anything. Salvation has little direct influence on their financial affairs. Some even gain earthly possessions when they follow Christ in Christian service. This point is well illustrated by the number of Christians and Christian ministers who have become members of the ecclesiastical jet set. They may be the heads of well-endowed Christian institutions or generous churches that supply them with large homes, new cars, trips around the world, and even private jets. You may wonder how these Christians interpret Jesus' teachings on riches. Indeed, Christians interpret Jesus' advice to the rich young ruler with varying levels of understanding. No doubt you and I and thousands of other Christians will continue to struggle with its meaning for centuries to come.

Perhaps as Christians we are called to a life of sacrifice and service. You may not feel led to a rigorous ascetic life-style. Jesus may not call everyone to that type of radical disciple-ship. But we can look to and learn from those who have indeed given up all of life's treasures to answer God's call. By putting less value on money and material possessions, you can begin to detach yourself from them. You may begin to think of them less as a means of security, and to use them more wisely. The purpose of this book is (1) to encourage you to think of money as a means or a tool of service, and not as an end in itself; (2) to suggest how you can use money more wisely and keep it from using you.

The Problem of Unbridled Consumerism

It sometimes seems that Christians and non-Christians alike share a common love affair with money. You and I live in a society of fanatic consumers. It's the American way of life to consume. How often have I paid the last installment on an item only to find another one to go in debt for! Through advertising and other means, manufacturers strive to make us feel less contented with what we have; they dupe us into believing we need more of everything—bigger, better, and the latest model.

The Dominating Dollar

Coming to terms with the dominating dollar is not easy. As you look at your own life, do you find you spend a third of your waking hours working for a paycheck? When you're offered a financially advantageous job somewhere else in the country, do you pick up your family and possessions and move there for a position that offers nothing more than money? Do you find your work demeaning to your character? Does it hurt your Christian witness? Or are you emotionally unfulfilled and unchallenged in your job? Mark Short quotes Joseph Sizoo, who once wrote: "In making a living today, many no longer leave room for life." And he adds: "It has been a continuing observation that many people in the business community are so intent on making a living that they have completely failed to live." (Mark Short, Jr., *The Bible and Business*, p. 9.)

As you evaluate your work habits, are you spending more time making a living than you are living and enjoying life? If so, you can do something about it. You can find another job, one that will bring joy to your working hours, one that you can look forward to each day. If you are presently unable to quit your job and find another one, you can be on the lookout for one in the near future. Forget about the job that will impress the world. Don't worry about climbing the ladder to success. You will have found your success when you find the job you enjoy, whether the paycheck is large or small. For you may be trading your entire lifetime, perhaps even ruining your health, for the power to consume. And you may fail to enjoy the exchange. Perhaps the things you buy no longer bring happiness and satisfaction. Truly, yesterday's luxuries have become today's necessities. In the United States, the standard of living since World War II has doubled. It seems that needs and wants, which have become almost inseparable, are always slightly greater than incomes. Could it be that you and I no longer possess possessions, but that they possess us? Arthur Gish puts it bluntly. Possessions "grow on us, obtain power over us, and become our master. . . . Possessions are like fire. They are good servants but cruel masters." (Arthur G. Gish, *Beyond the Rat Race*, p. 92.) That is a disturbing thought!

Money—The Most Unsatisfying of Possessions

Is your life geared for consumption, but not for living? Plato stated that most social evils can be traced to the possession of private property. When money dominates your life, your outlook on life may change. You may become resentful and jealous of those who have more than you do. You can spend every waking moment, and some sleeping ones, planning on how to make it, how to spend it, and how to protect it. J. C. Ryle believes that "money . . . is one of the most unsatisfying of possessions. It takes away some cares, no doubt; but it brings with it quite as many cares as it takes away. There is the trouble in the getting of it. There is anxiety in the keeping of it. There are temptations in the use of it. There is guilt in the abuse of it. There is sorrow in the losing of it. There is perplexity in the disposing of it." (Quoted in K. F. W. Prior, *God and Mammon*, p. 25.) Perhaps you will agree with him.

In our society, you and I live in the shadows of safe-deposit boxes, insurance policies, and locked windows and doors. You may walk the neighborhoods in fear that what you own might be snatched from you. Perhaps you even keep a distrustful eye on a fellow Christian who through some ulterior motive might seek to rob you of your property. That is the fear money evokes. That is one evil of money. We cannot escape the power and influence of the almighty dollar. It follows us everywhere, perhaps even into our religion and our church. With stewardship drives held often, with fund-raisers for new and bigger church buildings, and with radio, television, and pulpit preachers expounding on God's blessings poured out in the form of riches, we may have a difficult time getting away from the subject of money, even as we try to worship. I know of one popular black preacher who is rather blatant in his preaching on money and personal wealth. He instructs his radio congregation to send in their dollars in order to receive God's bountiful blessings—blessings which result in bigger houses and cars. This preacher refers to himself not as a *black* preacher, but as a *green* preacher, and claims that when the powerful green paper dollar speaks everybody listens. Needless to say, white preachers can be green preachers as well!

How can you escape the power and influence of the ever-dominating dollar? Perhaps you can strive to change your ideas about money. Close your ears to the voices of society—voices that tell you money equals success. Resist the urge to consume. Try to find contentment in things other than what money can buy: in your family, in your faith, and in yourself. Perhaps the goal of life is not to *have*, but to *have not*. In our current culture, this goal would require much more discipline and strength.

The Loss of Money

I believe one of the saddest aspects of material attachment, of unbridled consumerism, is the path of destruction it can leave in the lives of those who cannot control it. How many people do you know who find their happiness, their purpose in living, and their identity wrapped up solely in the size of their bank accounts? During the last few years, we have witnessed repeatedly the collapse of lives and of families as our nation has experienced economic depression and recession. All this suffering has been caused largely by the loss of employment, possessions, and money.

The New Poor

Almost every morning and evening, on local and national news programs and in newspapers, we see pitiful pictures and hear or read interviews with people who have become victims of our economy. Termed "the new poor," they are people who formerly owned homes and farms, paid taxes, sent their children to private day-care centers and schools, and were part of the blue- and white-collar work force. Many have lost all their possessions, have declared bankruptcy, have become involuntarily poor, and have moved into tiny apartments, old cars, tents, or campers, or live on the city streets. For them, loss of possessions, the indignity of losing a job, and the necessity of withdrawal from the consumer's market have left wounds that cut deeply into personal dignity and self-respect. And the unemployment figures continue to be high. At this writing, more than 11 percent are jobless in this country. Some estimate that the figure should be much higher, more realistically around 16 percent. Many unemployed workers have long since given up on finding another job. Some no longer file for unemployment checks. Countless others have adapted permanently to their new life-style.

Unemployment and Family Crisis

What the nation's unemployment problem has done to the family is an area of concern for you and me and other Christians. "Of the nation's 60 million families, 2.3 million families at present have no wage earner who is working. Another 4.8 million families have one wage earner who is unemployed." (Larry Braidfoot, "Strengthening Families and the Economic Crisis," *Light*, Jan.-Feb. 1983, p. 11.) While many have already lost their jobs, many more daily express the fear that they may be next. According to a recent Gallup poll, 8 percent of America's workers fear they will be unemployed within the next year. The frustration of losing a job and the fear of being next on the company's ax list have caused considerable distress in the family. Social workers and agencies have reported sharp rises in spouse and child abuse in the home. Just how many marriages have been broken, children hurt and even murdered, friendships lost, alcohol and drug addicts created, and health-care measures neglected because of a sudden loss of money and possessions cannot be estimated with certainty. Is money, indeed, a necessary evil? Looking at these statistics, you may agree that money does seem to be necessary in our society. And the loss of money, in most cases, does seem to cause havoc. Kierkegaard speaks harshly of money and possessions: "Riches and abundance come hypocritically clad in sheep's clothing, pretending to be security against anxieties, and they become then the object of anxiety, of 'the anxiety'; they secure a man against anxieties just about as well as the wolf which is put to tending the sheep secures them . . . against the wolf." (Quoted in Vernard Eller, *The Simple Life*, p. 103.) Considering the anxieties brought

about by the loss of money in this society, you may believe
Kierkegaard to be right.

Perhaps you have also been affected by the present economy. Have you recently lost your job? Are you struggling to
live on what is left in your savings account? Or are you trying
to support your family on low unemployment benefits,
government checks, or maybe no income at all? There are no
simple solutions for you. As you well know, recovery may
take a long time. But may you always trust in God and receive
courage from him as you journey through this difficult phase
of your life. May you realize that the loss of money can often
be determined by exterior forces, such as the nation's economy, and that loss of money does not mean loss of dignity. The
preciousness of your personhood does not come and go with
your pocketbook. I pray that, during these hard times, you
can draw strength from the treasures of life that no amount of
money can buy—from your own good health, from a loving
family and caring friends, and from your faith.

I realize that the above suggestions won't put food on your
table. Perhaps more concrete suggestions would be the
following:

1. Become involved in a concerned and loving Christian
community. You may find this community in your present
church home. Look to this group for emotional support.

2. Enlist the prayers of others. I believe that God truly
hears and answers prayers. Remember also to return the
prayers, and to pray for the needs of others who are having a
hard time.

3. Accept help when it is offered. This may mean "swal-
lowing your pride" temporarily. But very often the giver
receives a greater blessing than the one who receives. When
you are financially able, remember those kindnesses and help
those around you who suffer.

4. Keep meeting new people and thinking about new ways you can earn money. Do not remain stuck in one way of making a livelihood. Don't be afraid of starting over in life. A whole new chapter of life may open up to you.

The Value of Money vs. the Value of Human Life

How often the society in which you and I live puts money in a place slightly above human life. Perhaps daily you see and hear of living examples that confirm this culture's belief that people without real purchasing power are expendable: the unborn, the children, the poor, the "new poor," the handicapped, and the elderly. I am saddened when I hear of looters shot on sight in the midst of a citywide disturbance. How much more important is the person than the goods he or she may steal! I hurt each time a utility company turns off the electricity in the home of one who is unable to pay soaring energy bills. How many people, poor and elderly, have frozen in their beds at night for lack of heat?

Money versus human life. I sympathize with the anxious parents of a baby in Simpsonville, Kentucky—seven-month-old Laura Cay Boren. She was the victim of Severe Combined Immuno-Deficiency Syndrome, a potentially fatal blood deficiency disease. Doctors told her parents that without a bone marrow transplant, Laura could die in two or three months. But since Mr. and Mrs. Boren had no medical insurance and lacked the money to pay for the operation, they were refused entrance into the one hospital that held hope for the family— Duke University Hospital in Durham, North Carolina. Fortunately, and in barely enough time, several institutions and individuals in Kentucky and Indiana took pity on the young child. Together they contributed enough money to make this lifesaving surgery possible. Duke University officials agreed to admit Laura with a $20,000 deposit. But the doctors stated that this sum would cover only a portion of Laura's four-month hospital stay. In the face of criticism, and coming to the defense of the hospital, one doctor confessed: "I don't think that Duke are the bad guys. We all have to have money these days and Duke is no different."

The value of money versus the value of human life. Does that example sadden you? Do you ask, as I do: Is a baby's life not worth more than money? I cannot understand how anyone could let the precious Laura Cay Borens of this world suffer and die when the medical knowledge and equipment are available to save their lives.

Putting Money in Its Proper Place

As members of the present economic society, you may realize, as I do, that some money is necessary. You must be able to buy those things which sustain your life and that of your family. But acquiring a love for money is something quite different. It is an act that interferes with your relationship with God. It may close your eyes to the needs of others or create the desire for false needs. It can make you search endlessly for the glass slipper—the illusive American success story. Perhaps Jesus calls you and me to a different way.

What This Book Is Aimed to Do for You

In the following pages, I want to get down to specific nuts and bolts of your own spiritual decision about yourself as a consumer. How can you learn to be knowledgeable and responsible in your daily consumption and in your ownership of possessions? How can you live a life that puts Christ first and shows concern for your brothers and sisters in need? In essence, how can you live productively and creatively as a Christian in the way you earn, spend, save, and invest your money? I will offer suggestions to you, not as one who has found all the answers, but as a fellow struggler, a Christian who wants to live the best Christlike life possible. Together let us ponder Jesus' meanings about money and consumerism, and struggle to find understanding.

Chapter 2

Advertising—
Your Deceptive Hypnotist

In a way that you are not aware of, you are being brainwashed. The villain is clever and imaginative. He will use almost any means to entrap you. His methods are sometimes dishonest. This skilled manipulator aims to control you, and uses tricks and gimmicks that may catch you unawares. He repeats his propaganda again and again, often causing you to stare glassy-eyed and entranced at his subtle messages. Who is this deceptive hypnotist? The advertiser.

Of course, not all advertisers are deceptive. Some helpfully inform us and show us where to buy the products we truly need and how to save money on them. That kind of advertising needs little said about it, as its results are good. But some advertisers are not so helpful. The multibillion-dollar advertising industry consists of professionals who study your behavior, watch your buying habits, and then, often through cunning means, seek to sell you products that waste your money and even harm your health. These are the advertisers on which I will focus this chapter.

The Consumerism Trap

As a Christian consumer, you must become aware of these manipulators. Only by becoming aware can you resist their hooks on you and become a more responsible consumer.

I will confess to you. I am a child of the advertising explosion which made its dramatic, devious debut in the early 1950s. By the time I had reached the age of four, I had already been successfully drawn into the consumerism trap—the "I want it" syndrome. Through advertising directed toward the youngsters in my age group, the Davy Crockett craze of 1955 offered more than 300 different products, and added records and coonskin caps to my toy box. Indeed, my parents, when confronted by their demanding consumer daughter, contributed heavily to the $300 million Davy Crockett enterprise.

I am a product of many years of propaganda produced by teams of highly sophisticated technicians trained in human exploitation. I have been oblivious to their methods of insidious mastery. Their loud and clear messages have demanded that I look, hear, taste, smell, feel, and become quite involved with the products they produce. Consider this: I rise each morning and brush my teeth with the toothpaste promised to give me "sex appeal." I gargle with the mouthwash guaranteed not to give me "medicine breath." The deodorant I use is "strong enough for a man, but made for a woman." I use the most popular brand of makeup, shampoo, perfume, and soap. The clothes and shoes I buy are not necessarily comfortable or flattering, but are currently in fashion.

Truly, I am a victim of the advertising industry. I've come a long way since coonskin caps, but nevertheless, the consumerism road to my adulthood has been cluttered with unneeded products that guaranteed me results largely unfulfilled.

Why Do You Buy What You Buy?

Perhaps you have also purchased products that you didn't need, things that didn't live up to their intended purpose. You now wonder why you spent your money on them. The special brand of soft drink did not bring you the promised vitality, youth, and friends. The brand-name aspirin you took for a headache did not establish more loving relationships with your mother-in-law, your spouse, or your children. The hair color you bought did turn you into a blonde, but did not make you exciting, romantic, and popular.

Just why do you buy the things you buy every day? Why do you buy breakfast cereal loaded with sugar that provides abundant calories and little nourishment? Could it be that you too are a victim of intensive advertising campaigns? John Kenneth Galbraith writes that the central function of advertising "is to create desires—to bring into being wants that previously did not exist" (*The Affluent Society,* p. 129). The deceptive hypnotists are ever ready to create bigger and better desires, to plant unrealistic dreams in your head, and then to pounce on you unexpectedly through television, magazine, newspaper, and billboard ads. They employ every bit of technology they know for just one reason: to sell you their products. They wear you down with repeated messages, emotional music, subliminal symbols, and other means that work together to put you into a receptive mood. Then the hypnotists move in on you. They tell you to buy potato chips with ridges instead of potato chips without ridges. They tell you to buy the soft drink that claims to be "the real thing" instead of the supposedly imitation soft drink. Sitting in front of these electronic hypnotists, you soak in their message, rush out and buy the product, and then wonder why you bought it.

The Hypnotist Surrounds You

Television advertising isn't the only seductive type there is. The advantage of television, of course, is the means for sound and sight. Radio advertising comes in a close second. Through well thought out words, repetition, and clever jingles, radio is also a good route for advertisers. Magazine and newspaper ads, billboards, and the junk mail you receive each day also produce the desired results. The hypnotist even shows up in our supermarkets. Did you ever wonder why the makers of consumer products spend untold amounts of money on package design? Because the packaging lures you to buy them. Do you go into a supermarket with a list and come out with $60 more in merchandise than you had planned on buying? There's a reason for that.

In the mid-1950s, a study was made by James Vicary, a motivational analyst, to find out why shoppers bought so heavily on impulse. He suspected that some special psychology must be going on inside the shoppers as they walked through the stores. He set up a hidden motion picture camera that would record the eye-blink rate of customers as they shopped. How fast a person blinks his or her eyes is a good index of the state of inner tension. Vicary noted that the average person blinks 32 times a minute. Under extreme tension the rate increases to 50 or 60 times a minute. But if the same person is relaxed, the eye-blink rate may drop to a subnormal 20 or less. Vicary's test results startled him. The shoppers' eye-blink rates did not rise to indicate tension as they shopped. Instead they dropped to a very subnormal 14 blinks per minute! They developed a glassy stare as they moved up and down the aisles. Vicary surmised that these shoppers, as they passed through rows and rows of cleverly designed packages, would fall into a hypnoidal trance, a light kind of trance that is the first stage of hypnosis. (Vance Packard, *The Hidden Persuaders,* pp. 91–92.)

As a Christian consumer, be careful to resist impulse buying. When you go shopping, carry a detailed list so that impulse buying won't be a problem. Close your eyes as you buggy down the grocery store aisle. Pay no attention when bright boxes "scream" for you to buy them. Stay in the store only as long as necessary to buy your shopping-list items, for the longer you stay surrounded by the fancy packages, the harder it is to resist their charms. Realize that the rack displaying candy, chewing gum, and magazines will be greeting you at the cash register. These items are especially tempting if you must wait in the checkout line. Remember that stores put "impulse" items in a certain place just so you will notice them. The authors of *How to Live on Your Income* explain: "Candy and health and beauty aids are considered the top 'impulse' items. They are usually placed in those areas of the store where customer traffic is heaviest: candy (on lower shelves, for the convenience of children) with cookies and crackers, beauty aids near the dairy department. Items in special displays at the end of the aisle tend to increase impulse buying. Here you'll usually find special foods, discontinued products, magazines and hosiery." (Reader's Digest Association, *How to Live on Your Income,* p. 294.) Resist the temptation to buy on impulse.

Why Advertising Sells

Michael Lawrence and Terry Brandon aptly describe the lure of the ads on television: "It's a new day coming, but in a world that never existed . . . by folks who don't really live

there, a six-billion-dollar dream world created all for you. . . .
Television commercials—who can resist the promise of a new
day, a fresh start, and the product that just might make it
happen?" (Michael R. Lawrence and Terry Brandon, *The 30-
Second Dream* [film]; Lawrence Brandon Seider Film Produc-
tions, Inc., 1977.)

You can turn on your television set at any hour of the day
and be bombarded with high-powered commercials. A highly
sophisticated advertising industry goes to work on you,
without embarrassment and without conscience. The advertisers would have you believe that the solution to all your
problems is just a product away. Television advertising is a
dream world created just for you. You've probably grown up
with it, and even more frightening, you've grown used to it,
having accepted it as part of your life-style.

You probably no longer question how unrealistic advertising is—the talking animals; the children, propelled by bubble
gum, flying through the air; the carefully staged family
situations. The advertisers make it all seem so real, a dream
world much better than yours, where all things are possible if
only you buy their product.

What can you do about silly and unrealistic advertising?
Laugh! You can laugh at the absurd commercials you see and
hear every day. Only because of years of conditioning are you
able to watch with a straight face the woman who scrubs her
kitchen floor in her Sunday dress, or the interviews (supposedly filmed by a "hidden camera") of people who choose one
soft drink over another, or the extreme excitement generated
within a family over the type of fabric softener used on their
clothes. Those commercials are unrealistic, stupid, and funny!
You should treat them accordingly.

Did you know that "in an average lifetime [you will] spend
the equivalent of six years' full-time employment watching

television commercials. Americans spend six billion dollars a year—over $100 per family of four—for 'free television.' " (Lawrence and Brandon, *The 30-Second Dream.*)

How can you escape advertising on commercial television? One way might be to watch less commercial television. Change your television-watching habits. Instead of leaving your television set on for an indefinite length of time, choose carefully the programs you and your family will watch. While you will still be inundated with commercials, you will be enduring only those advertisers who interrupt your favorite programs. For a complete rest from commercials, watch public television. You may find, as I have, the quality of programming much improved, and you will not be in the direct line of fire of the advertisers.

The Dream World

Beware of advertising that plays on your emotions. If the greeting-card commercials bring tears to your eyes, if you begin to tap your foot to the snappy beat of a beer commercial, or if you find yourself longing for one of the babies with scrubbed faces in the diaper ads, then beware. You're about to become hooked. The advertisers are working on your emotions—your inner feelings. They aim to play on your weaknesses, anxieties, and frailties. Either decide not to look at them, or be consciously aware of their intentions.

Television advertisers tell you just what you want to hear. "We would all like to believe in the dream—family, intimacy, vitality, success—four areas of deep emotional concern where many commercials focus their promise." (Lawrence and Brandon, *The 30-Second Dream.*) Do you want to be loved and respected by your family? Then you must buy them a certain kind of toothpaste, serve them the snap-crackle-pop breakfast cereal, or cover them excessively with insurance policies.

According to advertisers, if you provide these things, your
family will look up to you, admire you for your wisdom, look
to you for protection. And, best of all, they will love you. It's
a mighty mean mama who won't buy her family heavily
sugared, tooth-decaying doughnuts for breakfast! Advertisers
would have you believe you owe it to your family to give
them the newest junk food or the latest computer toy. And
who in our society doesn't yearn to be loved and respected
and part of a family?

Intimacy

Intimacy is another area to which advertisers give their
utmost attention. They want you to believe that by using the
right soap, shampoo, or shaving cream, you will miraculously
find Mr. or Ms. Right. Advertisers go one step beyond
intimacy and into fantasy. If you drink a certain beer loaded
with "gusto," or smoke a certain brand of cigarette, you will
become masculine, virile, and popular with women. If you
use a particular perfume, a knight in shining armor will ride
into your kitchen and take you away from the dirty-dish
drudgery of everyday life. And who in our society doesn't
long for someone with whom to be intimate? Who doesn't
dream of an end to routine and an escape into a fantasy
world?

Vitality

Perhaps the dream of vitality is the most misleading. No
product can produce eternal health, attractiveness, and youth.
Yet advertisers claim that if you take an assortment of their
vitamins, drink the most popular beverage, or eat charbroiled
instead of fried hamburgers, you will soon be joining the
throngs of television "dream people"—people who overnight

become champion bowlers, swimmers, and volleyball players simply because they used that particular product.

Who in our society doesn't long to be free from pain, to be healthy and active? We want to "plop-plop, fizz-fizz" and have "fast, fast relief"—no waiting, no fuss or bother, but an immediate cure for whatever ails us. Through the use of robust teenagers, who supposedly represent society, advertisers have made you fearful of graying hair and advancing age. We may spend our lifetimes searching for the miracle preparation that will remove the wrinkles of time from our faces—all to somehow escape from the "sin" of getting older. Eternal youth and vitality are indeed a dream world.

Marks of Achievement

What do you associate with success in this society? Advertisers want you to believe that unless you own an expensive car or home, or the latest gadget, you are not successful. You are an achiever only if you have the necessary items to impress others, whether they be designer jeans or the right credit cards.

Do you spend your money on cars too big (or too small), on clothes, on vacations, on any number of things, not because you want them, but because you want to be surrounded by these marks of achievement—achievement according to advertisers?

Perhaps you, along with many others, think of possessions as marks of achievement. Advertisers are masters at distorting our views and our sense of values. And unless you stop them for yourself, your children will probably also learn to measure their own success by what they are able to buy. As a Christian consumer, you must be aware of advertising tricks. Propaganda is a method used to influence people to believe certain ideas or to follow certain courses of action. Advertising is propaganda. Be aware that advertisers use ideas and symbols you will feel deeply about: family, love, intimacy, health, vitality, success. Realize that these themes are being repeated again and again to appeal to your emotions. Turn the television set off during the commercials, or lower the volume so you will not be so easily captivated by their trickery. Refuse to become a victim of these untruthful propagandists.

You must also know what you are buying. When you buy orange juice, you are buying the juice of an orange, not energy, vitality, and liquid sunshine. Complexion soap will make you clean, but it will not bring you everlasting beauty. New cars will furnish you with transportation; they will not make you happy, amorous, and successful. A soft drink might quench your thirst, but it will not bring you instant friends and continuous volleyball games. Perfume will make your body smell perfumed, it will not bring you love, romance, and fairy-tale settings.

When you buy a product, beware of promises of instant happiness. Those are the thirty-second dreams that usually don't come true.

Advertising Exploitation

In various and misleading ways, some advertisers seek to exploit you. They promise you unrealistic dreams. They confront you at mealtimes with tempting pickles-lettuce-onions-cheese dripping from giant burgers. They create special days of the year, such as "Grandparent's Day," to sell you more greeting cards. Advertisers want to control you for the sake of selling you their products.

Your Children—"Consumer Trainees"

Probably the most dishonest act of advertising is its manipulation of young minds. Supposedly, adults can see a product or a commercial and have the wisdom and experience to reject it. But a child cannot.

With their expertise in brainwashing techniques, advertisers are spending millions of dollars trying to shape your children into their future consumers. In not too long a time, your little ones will be buying products they do not need, products that hurt their health, because for years they have been deliberately conditioned to do so.

Neil Postman, professor of "media ecology" at New York University, has estimated that "children in America see 750,000 television commercials during the formation period of their lives from 6 to 18." (Fred W. Graham, "America's Other Religion," *The Christian Century,* March 17, 1982, p. 306.)

Your children are now being indoctrinated to accept every new advertiser's trickery, to believe in a fantasy world, to consider themselves incomplete without the product being advertised. They are exposed daily to the dangers of advertising—to unfair stereotyped roles, to violence, and to irresponsible sex. According to Doris Longacre: "Our children's values are programmed through television commercials just as surely as they would be if they chanted political lines in nursery school. . . . We submit daily to brainwashing by commercial interests that must be equal to, if not more powerful than, the political posters and slogans of totalitarian governments." (Doris Janzen Longacre, *Living More with Less,* p. 53.)

By pouring money into the child and youth markets, advertisers can develop a certain brand loyalty among their young viewers and thus in time create a whole new flock of devoted adult consumers. They hook your children, their "consumer trainees," while your back is turned. As stated by Vance Packard: "If you expect to be in business for any length of time, think of what it can mean to your firm in profits if you can condition a million or ten million children who will grow up into adults trained to buy your product as soldiers are trained to advance when they hear the trigger words 'forward march' " (*The Hidden Persuaders,* p. 136).

Why do you as a parent, why do I as a parent, allow this brainwashing to continue day after day? If our children were being manipulated by religious cults or political activists, we would set off a parental storm of protest. So why are our children considered legitimate prey in the world of commerce? Probably because since our own childhoods you and I have also been the targets of conditioning and advertising propaganda. It has just become a way of life.

Teach your children about advertising. Watch commercials with your children and explain to them how that particular manufacturer is striving to sell them a toy or a snack. Teach your children to be aware of subliminal tricks, of the excessive use of sex and violence in ads, and of other subtle techniques. Laugh with your children when an unbelievable situation occurs in advertising, and let them know that this is not true to life—it is only make-believe and not to be taken seriously. Help your child not to become a "consumer trainee" for irresponsible consumerism in the future.

Sex and Violence

Advertisers depend heavily on sex and violence to sell products. Sex is routinely used to sell you everything from grass seed to gelatin. How can the fragrance of a particular perfume make you mysterious or innocent or sexy? By connecting a product with a scantily clothed young model, advertisers not only catch your eye, they can also make their product more appealing. You will begin automatically to associate a certain make of car with a model wearing black leather clothes. For some reason, sex sells in our society.

Violence also sells products. Maybe you, like millions of others, are drawn to the death-defying race car drivers as they circle a track at 200 miles an hour, or the sky diver who jumps thousands of feet from an airplane. These and other stunts are used repeatedly by advertisers who know that death appeals to the populace. One manufacturer noted that the caution label, now stamped on every pack, which exposes cigarettes as cancer-producing and dangerous, actually attracted more smokers.

Just what does the excessive use of sex and violence in advertising do to the minds of adults and impressionable children? Perhaps only time will tell.

Subliminal Advertising

First introduced back in the mid-1950s, subliminal advertising was developed by James Vicary, whose motivational study of shoppers was mentioned earlier. He used the principle that the mind actually records many impressions that the eyes and ears do not consciously see or hear. This type of advertising penetrates beneath your level of awareness to influence and manipulate you.

The next time you see an ad that particularly appeals to you, look at it closely. It may seem quite ordinary at first. But upon examination you may be able to pick out subliminal symbols. Your subconscious has already discovered them. Your "inner eye" is much quicker than your conscious eye.

In an ad, people and products and backgrounds are often arranged in a particular way for a particular reason. Subliminal symbols may be present in background clouds, or ocean water, or wrapping paper, or ice cubes in a glass of liquor. Some advertising artists have been known to airbrush faint images of objects into the copy, producing pictures and symbols of death, violence, and sex. They quickly pass by your conscious mind, but have a direct impact on your subconscious. And for reasons you are not aware of, these ads appeal to you and cause you to buy the products.

Be aware of advertising tricks. Pick out and evaluate the ads that use sex, violence, and subliminal symbols to sell you. Learn to spot the reasons why an ad appeals to you, and how it strives to manipulate you to buy.

Cheating the Very Poor

Advertising exploitation is not only unfair, it can be very cruel. When deceitful advertisers use their tricks on those who cannot afford to buy basic food and supplies, such as those living in underdeveloped countries, the results can be disastrous. This is especially true when the products that manufacturers advertise have no nutritional value.

The authors of *Food First* report that advertisers often reach children in underdeveloped countries by using toy gimmicks. In Mexico, General Foods put a plastic Walt Disney figure in packages of Jell-O—a product which they state has no nutritional value—and "encouraged kids to aspire to be 'the first to collect all 24.' " The results? "In one test market Jell-O sales jumped 1000 percent in one week." (Frances Moore Lappe and Joseph Collins, *Food First: Beyond the Myth of Scarcity,* pp. 303–304.)

In other underdeveloped countries, advertisers appeal to uneducated mothers who buy the products and feed them to their children. If these products have no food value, serious undernourishment can result. Again, the authors of *Food First* report: "In Zambia babies have become malnourished because their mothers fed them Coke and Fanta, believing it is the best thing they can give their children. . . . Dr. Stevens, the only pediatrician, reports that 54 percent of the seriously malnourished children admitted to the Children's Hospital at Ndola have 'Fanta Baby' written on the progress charts at the foot of their beds. The Zambian government now has reportedly banned Fanta advertisements 'because of their influence on the poor.' " (Lappe and Collins, *Food First,* p. 307.)

They conclude: "What a global food company . . . has to offer undeveloped countries is not good food but good advertising" (p. 303).

As a concerned Christian consumer, you can protest the use of unfair advertising on unsuspecting victims worldwide. You can learn more about advertising practices, write letters opposing such manipulation, keep abreast of current advertising in underdeveloped countries, and alert others to the problem.

Old vs. New-Improved-Bigger-and-Better

If you are like millions of other people in this society, you probably don't keep cars, appliances, or clothes until they wear out. You sell, give away, or otherwise dispose of older items even though they may work well. Why? Advertising may not be completely responsible for your disposal of things still serviceable, but it certainly could be a major influence.

How can manufacturers sell you something you do not need or something you already have? By making you feel you need whatever is new and improved, bigger and better. They urge you to discard your "out-of-date" goods and buy the "latest" style. Thus they keep you in long consumer lines at their cash registers.

Alvin Toffler states it simply: "The consumer is sometimes caught in a carefully engineered trap—an old product whose death has been deliberately hastened by its manufacturer, and the simultaneous appearance of a 'new improved' model advertised as the latest heaven-sent triumph of advanced technology" (*Future Shock*, p. 62).

Advertisers aim to keep you discontented so that you will always be ready to buy the next product they send your way. Have you ever noticed the words that keep appearing on name-brand products: new, improved, better, faster-acting, enriched. The manufacturers put these bright labels on everything from shampoo to floor wax. Each year they tell you they have made improvements on products that, according to their past claims, were already better than any competitor's product!

John Keneth Galbraith points out that manufacturers, "to create the demand for new [products], must contrive elaborate and functionless changes each year and then subject the consumer to ruthless psychological pressures to persuade him of their importance" (*The Affluent Society*, p. 232). And, as dishonest as that seems, you and I continue to fall for their gimmicks and buy their new, improved, better, faster-acting, and enriched products!

What can you do? You can choose not to be persuaded. If you do not need a product, don't buy it. Just because the manufacturers bring out a new or improved product and tell you that you must have the latest and greatest, don't take their word for it and rush out and buy that product. Don't let these "merchants of discontent" dictate to you what kind of car to drive, clothes to wear, or appliances to own. If you already have it, if it still works, and if you are satisfied with it, don't let yourself be pressured into replacing it. And if you don't need it in the first place, don't buy it, no matter how much the manufacturers say you need it.

Women and Drugs

Women are prescribed "more than twice the amount of drugs as men for the same symptoms. And that's true of all drugs," states Dr. Phyllis Irvine, associate professor of nursing at Ohio University. (Reported by Carol Cancila, in *The Courier-Journal,* Louisville, Ky., Sunday, May 1, 1983, p. H12.) Largely through commercials on television and ads in magazines and medical journals, advertisers address themselves to every fear, anxiety, and tension you might suffer as a woman of today. Whether they focus on your feelings of depression, anxiety, or frustration, the results are the same: "Studies indicate as much as 70 percent of the nation's mood-changing drugs are prescribed to women" (ibid.).

Do you long to escape from noisy children, an uncooperative spouse, housework, in-laws, or the office? Then you are continually being offered a quick exit—in the form of a pill. Some mood-altering drugs can cause addiction; most have undesirable side effects.

Why are women given more prescriptions for moods than men? Russel Falck, program director for United Health Services, believes that as a culture, "society permits women greater expression of emotions . . . and that women are more likely than men to perceive emotional problems in themselves" (ibid.). Thus advertisers spend considerable time, energy, and money directing these drug ads to women rather than to men.

Physicians are also manipulated by advertising in medical journals. They may prescribe medications to take care of all sorts of problems that you, their female patient, may encounter. It often makes little difference whether you suffer from a serious malady or the blues and the blahs. According to Dr. Stephen England, a Dayton, Ohio, obstetrician and gynecologist: "It's a lot harder to talk to a person and spend an hour trying to draw out their problem when you can write a prescription" (ibid.).

By using female images in advertising, and by telling you

that you need these drugs, advertisers successfully market these medications. They continue to victimize you and other women who believe their ads.

As a woman, you must oppose these practices that make you and your female friends depend on drugs that alter your moods. When you visit your doctor, ask what pill he or she is prescribing, why you should take it, and what the results and side effects will be. Then decide for yourself whether the advantages outweigh the disadvantages. Ask yourself if you really *need* the drug, and whether you could get along without it. Don't just take a doctor's word for it; know what you are putting into your body.

Conclusion

While not all advertisers set out to deceive you, much of the advertising we see and hear is misleading. Advertising is produced by manufacturers who want to manipulate you. Through psychological and subliminal trickery, they strive to sell you their products. You must be on your guard for these hypnotists who enter your home and your mind, and who prepare your children to become adult consumers of their future products. These are the professional deceivers who play on your emotions and often use unscrupulous means to advance their products.

Clare Barnes, Jr., wrote: "Advertising has done more to cause the social unrest of the Twentieth Century than any other single factor." (Quoted in Vance Packard, *The Status Seekers,* p. 318.) As long as advertisers control you and me and other consumers like puppets on strings, they will continue to cause great social unrest. As a Christian consumer, you can be aware of their tactics, and you can alert others to beware. You can avoid their propaganda—their brainwashing gimmicks that catch you unawares. Through knowledge and deliberate resistance, you can help put an end to these deceptive hypnotists—the advertisers.

Chapter 3

Impressing Our Neighbor

Have you ever read the short story "The Necklace," by Guy de Maupassant? He writes of a very pretty but very poor young woman named Matilda, who lives in Paris with her husband, Loisel, a government clerk. Matilda feels she is better than her common caste. She longs for riches.

One day she and her husband receive an invitation to the Commissioner's ball—a gala event that would be attended by people much richer than they. With their savings of four hundred francs, Matilda buys a simple but elegant gown to wear. Still, she is not satisfied. "I am vexed not to have a jewel, not one stone, nothing to adorn myself with. I shall have such a poverty-laden look," she sighs to her husband. Then Loisel remembers one of Matilda's wealthy friends, Mme. Forestier, who was a schoolmate at the convent. She would have jewels for Matilda to wear. Matilda visits her friend and borrows a beautiful diamond necklace.

Matilda is a great success at the ball. She impresses all the guests with her beauty and the necklace. But on the way home Matilda loses the necklace. She and her husband search endlessly but never find it. They go from jeweler to jeweler and try to find an identical necklace to replace the lost one. Finally they locate one very similar, but at the cost of thirty-six thousand francs. Loisel signs notes, makes "ruinous promises," and "compromises his whole existence" to buy it. Matilda takes the newly purchased necklace to her friend without telling her what has happened.

For the next ten years, Loisel and Matilda must work day and night to repay the lenders. They know extreme poverty. They waste away their health. Matilda's beauty fades quickly with each passing day. Finally they repay the debt.

One Sunday, as Matilda walks along the Champs Elysées, she runs into Mme. Forestier. She decides to tell her friend about losing the necklace and working a decade to replace it. At the end of her confession, her friend grasps Matilda's hands and replies: "Oh! my poor Matilda! Mine were false. They were not worth over five hundred francs!" (Guy de Maupassant, "The Necklace," *The Complete Short Stories of Guy de Maupassant,* pp. 172–177.)

Does the irony of this story intrigue you? You will agree that Matilda paid dearly for the privilege of impressing the guests at the ball. Matilda's yearning to impress others affected not only her life but that of her husband. Loisel also had to pay the price. Matilda's pleasure lasted only a short time in comparison to the debt it cost her.

As I reread the story, something I find even more ironic than Matilda's plight is Mme. Forestier's lack of knowledge about the necklace. For ten years she owned a necklace worth much more than she could have imagined. Could the author be telling us that before she borrowed the necklace, Matilda also owned treasures far beyond her understanding? She had her home, her husband, her health, and few worries about overwhelming debts.

Of course, the story of Matilda and Loisel was created in the mind of the author. But how many times do you and I fail to appreciate the treasures we have? How often do we yearn for those things which will cause others to stop and admire us? The great American dream is not to be outdone by our neighbor. But you and I pay dearly for the privilege of impressing others.

Keeping Up with the Joneses

Christmas mornings were always such fun at my house. Mom and Dad made sure that my sister, Jill, and I awoke to a variety of toys. I remember one special little doll sitting in a miniature swing under the Christmas tree. It was love at first sight. She had blue eyes surrounded by plastic black eyelashes that opened and closed when I tilted her body. (If you have lived at least three decades, you will remember those "primi-tive" dolls who had not yet learned to walk, talk, roller-skate, and compute mathematical figures.) After breakfast, I rushed out to show her to my neighborhood girlfriends.

I was very satisfied with my blinking doll . . . until I saw the doll that Santa had brought my little friend. A Betsy-Wetsy! Betsy could drink water from a bottle and wet her diaper! I was impressed. After my friend let me change Betsy's wet pants a few times, my doll had lost all her appeal. I wanted a Betsy-Wetsy too.

You might agree that times haven't changed much in thirty years. I recently heard of two preschoolers arguing over whose home was larger. Today's youngster might be compar-ing computer accessories or talking calculators with his or her neighborhood friends. But the idea is the same: If you have one, I must have one too. It's called "keeping up with the Joneses." It is the spirit that demands what my neighbor has. Sometimes it will go one step farther. If my neighbor has one, then I've got to have one bigger, better, newer, and more impressive.

Do You Buy Things to Impress People?

Do you buy things, not because you really need them, but because your neighbor has them? Do you buy things to impress others? Do you long to acquire more prestige and status? Do you receive your self-esteem through your possessions? If you do, you are not alone. E. F. Schumacher writes: "The acquisition of wealth [has] become the highest goal of the modern world in relation to which all other goals . . . have come to take second place." (E. F. Schumacher, *Small Is Beautiful*, p. 277.)

In considering what you buy and why you buy, ask yourself these questions: Am I working *just* for a large paycheck? Did I buy my house primarily for its large size and prestigious location? Is my furniture more expensive than I could afford? What model of car do I drive and why? Do I dress to impress my co-workers, my neighbors, and my fellow church members? Where do I spend my vacations and why? Why do I send my children to the particular school they attend?

As I address those questions, I realize I have also fallen into the popular mood of the country. I would feel self-conscious walking down my neighborhood street in either a miniskirt or a maxiskirt, since both are currently out of style. Would my friends think I couldn't afford a more fashionable dress? And after my husband's student days, I was delighted to trade in our ten-year-old, 180,000-mile Plymouth for a new Pontiac.

Arthur Gish states: "Wealth does not satisfy. Gaining new possessions stimulates the desire for still more. . . . Striving for power, status, and prestige leads not to fulfillment, but frustration." He concludes: "When consumption becomes an end in itself, it not only places too high a value on things, but limits our ability to see the relationship of things to higher purposes." (Gish, *Beyond the Rat Race*, pp. 94–95, 96.)

The Real Cost You Pay to Impress Others

When you buy things only to impress people, the cost can be quite high. Several things can occur.

You Can Lose Friendships. By always striving to have more than your neighbor, you can lose his or her friendship. With your possessions you can create barriers between yourself and others, even your good friends. You can cause others to withdraw from you. You can destroy your sense of community with your neighbors.

In a sermon preached on Palm Sunday in 1909 at St. Nicolai's Church in Strasbourg, Albert Schweitzer gave the following example. He tells of visiting a woman who wanted to show him something in the attic of her building. But as she was about to leave her apartment, she hesitated and went back inside to fetch her key. She explained: "My door has a lock which cannot be opened from the outside. If I slam it shut, I lock myself out of my own apartment."

Dr. Schweitzer explained: "Through their own conduct, [people] often lock themselves out of the best that is within them. Only afterward do they realize how poor they have become. They have cut themselves off from the world of goodness and beauty within them." (Albert Schweitzer, *Reverence for Life,* p. 79.)

When you make a tremendous effort to keep up with your neighbor's buying habits, or when you try to acquire more for the sake of making an impression on your neighbor, you can lock yourself outside his or her friendship. Material attachments can be the door that separates you from your friend. The friend may never really get to know the more important qualities you possess, because your possessions stand in the way. How easy it is to "slam the door shut" by dwelling on things that, in the long run, do not impress anyone at all.

You Can Corrupt Your Neighbor. By trying to impress, we can cause our friends to covet what we have. The apostle Paul recognized the seriousness of covetousness. After describing his labors in God's work, he felt it important to add: "I coveted no one's silver or gold or apparel" (Acts 20:33). Without even knowing it, in your efforts to consume, you may be causing your neighbor to want what you have. Craving another's possessions is inseparable from resentment and jealousy. If your neighbor shares your material attitude, he or she must also work harder to keep up with you. The writer of Ecclesiastes calls this a "striving after wind": "Then I saw that all toil and all skill in work come from a man's envy of his neighbor. This also is vanity and a striving after wind. . . . There is no end to all his toil, and his eyes are never satisfied with riches, so that he never asks, 'For whom am I toiling and depriving myself of pleasure?' This also is vanity and an unhappy business" (Eccl. 4:4, 8).

You Can Corrupt Yourself. If you are an upward striver for material wealth, you can become addicted to buying. Material objects can enslave you. Instead of spending your money on more important things, such as meeting the needs of others, you can become a dreamer, always longing for the one possession not easily within your reach. Vernard Eller calls this a "slave march," observing that "masses of our contemporaries have become trapped into the slave march of making money and spending it—production, consumption, luxury, keeping up with the Joneses. We need a liberation movement here as much as in any other aspect of life." (Eller, *The Simple Life,* p. 58.)

Much of the striving for possessions is the yearning for power. Power-hunting can quickly consume you and dominate your life. It can cause you to think of yourself as superior to others of God's children. It can eat away your time, your energy, and your health. To maintain the image, you may be forced to make compromises. You can easily suffer from overwork and worry in your quest for wealth and power. Matilda knew the price of making an impression. She corrupted herself and emerged a broken woman with little to show for her troubles. When money becomes a priority in your life, when possessions become your main goal for living, you do yourself a great injustice. You cause yourself personal discontentment. For no matter how much you have, you will still want more. And you will always meet people who have more than you have. No doubt you will never feel you have enough if trying to impress others is your goal.

You Can Corrupt Your Relationship with God. Regular worship, maintaining an effective prayer life, and communing with God are things that take time and concentration. If you spend much of your time and thought on acquiring possessions, you can rob yourself of a meaningful relationship with God. Your spiritual needs and wants may be sacrificed in order to meet your material needs and wants. Your daily walk with God must remain unhindered by status-seeking and the collecting of material possessions.

Do you find yourself in Matilda's situation? Do you want to stop trying to impress others with your possessions and start to make a change? You can.

How to Step Off the Consumer Merry-Go-Round

First of all, change your thinking about possessions. They do not make you important. You are already important. You are a child of God, unique and individual. You do not need to hide behind gold and silver and the other things this society considers valuable. You have inner value. Television's Mr. Rogers tells his preschool audience daily: "I like you just the way you are." No doubt your neighbors could say that about you. They like you just the way you are, without all the things that interfere with your real value as a person.

Evaluate what you buy and why you buy it. If you truly need an item, if it can save you time and energy, and if you can afford it, then buy it. Some purchases are necessary. I have an antique washboard hanging on the wall of my back porch. It is adequate for decor, but I shudder to think of having to wash my clothes on it! My automatic washer saves me time and labor. For me, my washer was a necessary purchase.

If you want something not because you need it but because your neighbor has one, or because you could impress somebody by having one, then don't buy it. That possession is just what you do not need.

Take a good look at the people who truly impress you. Chances are, the new car in their driveway or the English porcelain in their china cabinet is not what impresses you. Perhaps their creativity, their caring for other people, their aim to be good parents or responsible church and community workers, is what you really admire. And what impresses you about them will also impress them about you.

Be careful not to allow society to dictate your actions. A secondhand furniture store recently announced it would deliver newly bought used furniture in an unmarked van. Your neighbors would not have to know you bought it at that particular store. No doubt some of your neighbors would be upset at the thought of your buying secondhand furniture. Those are the same neighbors who would not invite you to dinner or their country clubs as often if you asserted yourself as an individual and pulled out of their impressive circle. But do you really want friends who only value you for your valuables? Indeed, you can step off the consumer merry-go-round. It only takes your money and, for a short time, surrounds you with bright lights and exciting music. But it leads nowhere. It goes only in circles and eventually will stop for you to get off anyway.

The Burden of Unneeded Possessions

Consider the burden of having possessions you don't need. If you buy only to impress others, you will probably have much more than you can properly take care of. When you make a purchase, consider the amount of work involved: You must select it, work for the money to pay for it, buy extra insurance and more locks to protect it. Some possessions, such as small airplanes and boats, will need rented shelter space. You must keep your possessions clean, cared for, oiled, and repaired. After you have become dependent on them, when they wear out, you will have to replace them.

Material possessions can be a burden. Are they really worth the extra trouble? Could you not spend that time and energy more productively? If you really need the object, it may be worth the work. In some cases, however, even the labor-saving devices can make more labor for you. Indeed, possessions can easily rob you of your freedom. For the more you have, the less free you are.

What can you do with unneeded possessions? Get rid of them! Sell them. Give them away. Have a yard sale. Your junk may truly be treasure to someone else. You may find as you slowly diminish your possessions that they will mean less to you and your family. You will know a great freedom from them. You will have more time to use creatively. Perhaps one day you will wonder why you ever bought an electric can opener, an automatic popcorn popper, or an electric potato peeler. You will recall that these gadgets used energy unnecessarily and took up space in your cabinets. Assess your possessions. Do they cause you more work than they provide? If so, dispose of them. Before you buy anything else, ask yourself if it is honestly worth the money, time, and effort you must expend to own it.

Maintaining the Image—A Lifetime of Debt

Impressing our neighbor can cause serious financial problems. When buying to impress becomes an obsession, you may deprive yourself and your family of the basics of life. You may not have adequate funds to provide your children with nourishing food, warm clothing, and a good education because you keep an expensive sports car in your garage.

How many people do you know who have had a good job, and bought various things on credit, only to have that job and regular paycheck fall out from under them? Who pays the large credit debts then? If they can't be paid, what happens to the items bought on credit? Many times people lose what they were buying along with the money they have already invested. Overextended credit can also cause considerable tension between a husband and wife. With both working just trying to keep up with the bills, earning a paycheck may well become the main focus of their marriage as well as of their lives. And how many couples who wanted to have children have postponed or even canceled their plans to raise a family in order to get on their feet and out from under heavy debts?

In this day, buying on credit is a popular way to support an

image. The fact that you don't have the money does not mean
you can't purchase the item. But beware. The lure of easy
credit can be habit-forming and destructive.

The Uses and Abuses of Easy Credit

Whole books have been written on the topic of using credit
wisely. In the space of this chapter, I cannot delve very deeply
into the subject of credit use. But I do want to tell you of
ways that you, a Christian consumer, can use credit to your
benefit while at the same time avoiding its many pitfalls.

You probably have borrowed money in your lifetime. Fifty
years ago the American consumer had little to do with credit.
Purchases were made on cash-and-carry terms. Today, however, the use of credit is popular and widespread. Perhaps you
took out a loan from your bank, a small loan company, or a
credit union, or through your credit card company. That loan
may have been used to buy your house, your car, or to pay for
your college education. That loan may have been small, and
used for such things as home improvements or minor medical
emergencies. Wherever, however, or for whatever you borrowed the money, one thing is sure: you had to pay for the
use of it.

Credit offers many great advantages to you. Can you
imagine having to save enough money to buy a house before
you moved in? Or having to walk to work until you could save
money for a car? Perhaps you would have been unable to get
an education, or to educate your children, were it not for
credit loans. I have come to depend a great deal on credit.
Perhaps you have too. How can you use credit to your
advantage and not abuse it or be abused by it?

Installment Loans

Most people borrow money on the installment plan through banks. The bank lends you a large or small sum of money, and you agree to pay it back in small sums or installments over a period of time. For the use of the money, you pay the bank interest. Personal finance and small loan companies will also lend you money, and will usually take much greater credit risks than the bank. But they may charge higher interest rates and service charges. If you are a member of a credit union, you may be able to borrow money at a much lower rate of interest.

Some banks or companies will ask for collateral before they will lend you money. This might be property or securities pledged by you, the borrower, to protect the interests of the lender. If you have no collateral, you may be required to have a cosigner. That person will be responsible to the bank or loan company for seeing that the loan is repaid.

You may borrow money for a variety of reasons. The average American today borrows most to buy new cars, then used cars, and then major appliances, in that order. No matter what your reasons for borrowing money, you should take some precautions.

The Wise Use of Installment Credit

Always borrow from a reputable source. Shop around for the best terms and interest rates, as they vary from place to place.

Be careful not to overextend yourself. Just because you can borrow a large amount of money, don't be tempted to buy more than you need. Look at your overall monthly installment payments and judge whether you can afford the new purchase. Financial experts recommend that "twenty to twenty-five percent of one's income is the maximum amount that should be committed to installment debt." (James E. Kilgore, *Dollars & Sense*, p. 55.)

Before you sign any agreement with a loan officer, know the terms of the agreement. Read the contract and the small print. Ask questions. If you don't understand the financial language, don't be afraid to ask what it means in detail. While reading the contract, look for the following: the amount you want to borrow, the interest and/or service charges you must pay (in dollars and percents), the total amount due, the amount of each payment, and the date each payment is due. If you are buying a car or other item on the installment plan, look for the amount of the down payment, the trade-in allowance, and the insurance charges, if any. Also be sure there are no blanks left in the contract for the lender to fill in later.

If by some chance you should ever fall behind in your installment payments, call your loan officer and tell him the situation. If you have made your past payments promptly, and have established a good credit rating, perhaps he or she can help you work something out until you can continue paying on time.

Credit Cards

Are you an owner of that neat plastic card known as the credit card? Many different types of credit cards exist today. Some can be used at only one store. Others are more generally accepted. Some can even be used in countries throughout the world. Your little credit card can be of great advantage to you or it can get you into great trouble. It all depends on how you use it.

I have found, and perhaps you have too, that the advantages of the credit card are numerous. For one thing, you need not carry large amounts of cash with you when you

shop, travel, or eat out. The credit card saves time. You will
not have to run to the bank every time you need a few dollars.
It is convenient. Have you ever been asked out to lunch and
discovered your purse empty? Many restaurants will honor
some type of credit card. A card can also save money. You
can buy items now at today's prices and pay for them later.
Had you waited to save enough cash for that same purchase,
inflation would have made it cost more. In an emergency, you
can borrow money with your credit card. These loans are
called "cash advances" or "instant cash." In effect, every time
you use your credit card, you have the advantage of a short-
term loan without the hassle of filling out forms at a bank or
loan company.

But the credit card also has its disadvantages. You may
spend more money. "It has been found that credit card users
spend 30 percent more than cash customers." (Susan Allen,
Your Money's Worth, p. 52.) A credit card might be *too*
convenient! Some banks and credit card companies require a
service fee on top of interest charges for the use of their
credit card. I once paid $2.50 a month just for the use of a
major credit card. That did not include interest payments
when I failed to pay a bill on time. And some cards charge
interest from the date a purchase is made. The interest rates
on credit cards can be very expensive, sometimes ranging
from 18 to 22 percent or more. If you pay only the minimum
amount due when the bill arrives, and the balance is carried
over until the next bill, you will pay heavily for the use of the
money. If you own a card that charges interest from the date a
purchase is made, you will pay more money for each item you
buy just by using your credit card.

The Wise Use of Credit Cards

How can you use credit cards to your benefit? Here are a
few suggestions:

Shop around for a credit card that charges no service fee. I saved money each month when I found a bank that supplied the credit card service fee free. Also, check the rate of interest the credit card company or bank charges from the date of your purchase or in the event that you don't pay the entire balance upon receipt of the bill. You might also want to choose a credit card that is universally accepted. In this way you can depend more on one credit card rather than having several store-name cards that can be lost or stolen.

Borrow cash advances or instant cash only in an emergency. If possible, try to pay such loans back quickly. Be aware of any extra charges for borrowing sums of money with your credit card.

As with installment loans, judge the item carefully before you buy it. If you don't need it, don't buy it. Resist buying on impulse. A few dollars at a super sale and a few more dollars at a bargain table can add up quickly. Don't let the convenient credit card lure you into increased spending.

Pay the entire balance, if possible, within the credit card company's time frame. Many credit card companies, but not all, carry a billing date of twenty-five to twenty-eight days. On these cards, unlike some others, by paying the balance in full you will pay no interest charges at all.

If you find yourself over your head in bills on a credit card, call the bank or company that issued the card to you. Explain your situation. Ask for help. With interest rates high, the longer you delay the payment in full, the deeper in debt you will go. You may want to stop using your credit card until you can catch up on your past payments. Use cash for a while. If you find that you spend much less with cash than with your credit card, don't be afraid to keep the credit card in a drawer just for emergencies. You might even want to dispose of it altogether. Cut it up into small pieces, so that no one else could use it, and throw it away.

Credit can be a good way to buy now and pay later. By learning how to use credit properly, you can use it to your advantage. But the use of credit can also consume you and cause you much anxiety over high bills. Items can end up costing you more than you had expected if you allow bills to accumulate over a period of time. Decide how you will use credit and stick to your plan. And however you decide to use credit, be sure you buy for the right reasons. Buying to impress others might be more tempting with today's easy and available credit. But it still remains a dead-end street.

Conclusion

What do your material possessions say to others around you? The messages you may be sending out, even though unspoken, will be loud and clear. How you decide to spend your money tells others what kind of person you are. Your spending habits speak volumes. If you spend large amounts of money to buy the things your neighbor buys, just because your neighbor buys them, then you are buying for the wrong reasons. Keeping up with the Joneses is impossible. If you buy things only to impress others, then you are not being a responsible consumer.

Yearning to impress others might cost you more than you can imagine. You will spend much time and energy caring for your unneeded possessions. You can corrupt your neighbor by causing him or her to covet what you have. You can become a slave to material things and thus corrupt yourself. Your relationship with God might even suffer. And with today's easy credit you can go heavily in debt. The price you pay to impress might be very high for you and your family.

You could ruin your credit rating, create family tension, hurt your health from excessive fretting over bills, and even court bankruptcy.

As a Christian consumer, you must ask yourself: Is impressing my neighbor really worth the price?

Chapter 4

Christians in a Needy World

Would you like to know the best and most satisfying secret of spending your money wisely and carefully, and at the same time not becoming a miserly skinflint? The way to do it is to search out the unemployed and the poverty-stricken and use a generous portion of your money and goods to help them to have work and food, clothing and shelter. Then you will watch and spend the money you have left with more wisdom and care.

In his biography of Mother Teresa of Calcutta, entitled *Something Beautiful for God,* Malcolm Muggeridge includes a photograph of Mother Teresa holding a small Indian child. Her face is heavily lined and tired, yet nonetheless radiant. Her small, bent body reflects the many years of suffering she has endured on behalf of the sick and dying people of Calcutta. The dark-skinned child she holds snuggles close to her chest. Naked and already weary from the effects of poverty, he shows by his expression the love, acceptance, warmth, and complete contentment he has found in her arms.

I read this biography of Mother Teresa long before she became a Nobel Peace Prize winner. It describes how, as a young peasant girl of eighteen, she left her home in Yugoslavia to answer the call of God to be a nun. She took her final vows in Loreto in 1937 and was put in charge of a school in India. Then she received her second calling—her "vocation to the poor." She set out into the streets of Calcutta to serve the "poorest of the poor." In 1952, with the help of the sisters of the Missionaries of Charity, Mother Teresa opened the first Home for the Dying. Her first patient was a woman "half eaten by the rats and ants" she picked up from the street. Since then, Mother Teresa and the sisters have cared for more than 30,000 people from the poorest sections of Calcutta.

The sick, the lepers, the dying, the unwanted babies "picked out of dustbins." To all of these Mother Teresa ministers with a selfless love, a Christlike love. Malcolm Muggeridge writes in the preface of his book: "For me, Mother Teresa of Calcutta embodies Christian love in action. Her face shines with the love of Christ on which her whole life is centred, and her words carry that message to a world which never needed it so much." (Malcolm Muggeridge, *Something Beautiful for God,* Preface.)

Jesus and the Poor

Jesus had a selfless love for the poor. He ministered amid all the dirt and disease and misery in the world. You've probably read many times of the harsh criticism Jesus endured from the religious leaders of his day, all because he ate with, fellowshipped with, and identified with the poor and the oppressed. Jesus had great compassion on the unfortunate. He loved those whom the world despised. For he himself was a poor man. Jesus belonged to the poverty-stricken class. He had no place to be born and no earthly possessions; he took the lowly form of a servant (Phil. 2:7); and at his death he was buried in a borrowed grave. He knew hunger and physical suffering. As one of the poor, he had compassion for them. "Blessed are you poor," he preached, "for yours is the kingdom of God" (Luke 6:20). In this passage, Jesus echoed the old prophetic message: "Who is like the LORD our God, who is seated on high, who looks far down upon the heavens and the earth? He raises the poor from the dust, and lifts the needy from the ash heap" (Ps. 113:5–7).

Imagine. Jesus calls "blessed" the poor, the oppressed, the humble, and the suffering! He loves those who were rejected. In the end, he gives his life for them. "The Spirit of the Lord is upon me," Jesus said, "because he has anointed me to preach good news to the poor . . . , to proclaim release to the captives . . . to set at liberty those who are oppressed" (Luke 4:18).

The sick, the lepers, the dying, the unwanted babies picked out of trash cans—to such was the ministry of Jesus. And to such is the ministry of Mother Teresa and many like her, who identify with and minister to the poor of this world.

The Poor Are Always with You

You might agree that as far as the world's poor are concerned, things haven't changed much in two thousand years. Even with improved technology and knowledge, people around the world are still hungry, diseased, naked, and dying.

If you have not read them lately, the statistics on world poverty might shock you. The Food and Agriculture Organization of the United Nations estimates that "up to 450 million people suffer from severe undernutrition." ("The What and Where of Hunger," *Sprouts,* Nov. 1982, p. 4.) Another shocking statistic is that "750 million people in the poorest nations live in extreme poverty with annual incomes of less than $75." (Ronald J. Sider, ed., *Cry Justice! The Bible on Hunger and Poverty*, p. 1.)

In magazines, newspapers, and on television, you have probably seen the results of world poverty. Hunger, disease, death, lack of hygiene and medical services, bad living conditions, inadequate housing, lack of clothing—all caused by poverty. Did you know that in many underdeveloped countries half the children die before they reach the age of fifteen? And illiteracy abounds as children face a severe lack of schools and teachers. Nearly half the inhabitants of the world suffer from diseases linked with malnutrition, yet health care is almost nonexistent. "In the developed countries there is one doctor for every 1,000 inhabitants. In the poor countries, there is one doctor for every 10,000, 50,000 or even 70,000 inhabitants. France alone has more hospital beds than the whole of Asia." (Arthur McCormack, *World Poverty and the Christian*, pp. 19–20.)

Urgent Problems: Hunger and Malnutrition

Today's hunger problem is unique for several reasons. H. Davis Byrd writes: "Famine is now more a result of economics than geography. . . . The magnitude of famine is unequaled in human history. . . . For the first time in human history mankind has the resources available to eliminate hunger from the entire face of the earth." (H. Davis Byrd, "World Hunger and American Christians," *Religion in Life*, Spring 1980, p. 49.)

Children are usually the first victims of hunger. In developing countries, one child in four dies before the age of five. Half of these deaths are caused by inadequate food. Death is slow for the hungry. Malnutrition steals their energy, retards their growth, and causes their brain to vegetate. And malnutrition begins long before a child's birth, for untold numbers of expectant mothers suffer from lack of nourishment during pregnancy. Inadequate food for the fetus may result in a low birth weight (a prime cause of infant death), or physical and mental problems—stunted growth, deafness, mental retardation, blindness, and a weakened resistance to disease.

I cannot imagine letting my toddler son miss one meal. Yet untold millions of mothers must watch as their young children go without food day after day and slowly starve to death. A magazine recently reported cases of families in India committing suicide together rather than die lingering deaths of starvation, and of distraught fathers throwing little children into rivers to drown rather than watch them starve to death.

Do you not ache for these mothers and fathers who are powerless to provide food for their families? Could you bear to stand by and watch your child starve to death? Surely, world hunger remains a problem that needs an immediate cure!

Why Do Some Eat While Others Starve?

Pope John Paul II presents the problem of world hunger today "with tragic urgency, because its solution, rather than becoming closer with the passing of time, seems rather to be getting further and further away." (Pope John Paul II, "The Poor Will Eat and Will Have Their Fill," *L'Osservatore Romano,* Aug. 2, 1982, p. 2.)

As a concerned Christian, you are probably also greatly distressed about world hunger. Food is the basic right of all of earth's citizens. I believe every human being has a right to his or her share of food, to human dignity itself. You and I, and all human beings, are created in the image of God. That gives value and worth to every living soul.

The reasons for world poverty are varied. They are certainly not simple. Poverty results from a mixture of things such as politics, economic inequality, energy crises, increased consumption, decreased consumption, natural disasters, and environment. The fact that politics and economics don't mix has been proved a number of times. Yet time and again, politicians delve into economics, and economists interfere in politics. The result is often a state of confusion that affects millions of people worldwide. Some experts state that technology has caused much poverty. As technology becomes more advanced, unskilled laborers in developing countries cannot compete with the rapid production of the Western world. Others believe that environment plays a big role in causing poverty. Those who live in the United States are blessed with highly productive soil, plenty of water, and a good growing climate. But not all countries are as fortunate. Much of the world's soil does not produce vegetation. Floods, famines, and other natural disasters also contribute to the loss of food production. Lack of fertilizer, irrigation, up-to-date equipment, and knowledge, combined with problems of import and export and land ownership, contribute too.

Some eat while others starve. You may agree that this is an unfair situation dependent on many factors. I shake my head in disbelief as I read one "explanation" of the worldwide distribution of poverty and wealth. Of impoverished people, the author notes: "This is how God controls heathen cultures: they must spend so much of their time surviving that they are unable to exercise ungodly dominion over the earth." And: "The third and fourth worlds are suffering under the judgment of God." (Quoted by Kenneth L. Gentry, *Fundamentalist Journal*, March 1983, p. 38, in a review of the book *Productive Christians in an Age of Guilt-Manipulators—A Biblical Response to Ronald J. Sider*, by David Chilton.) How sad that anyone should think this way. I would like to see the author explain his theological interpretations to a malnourished, diseased baby in Bangladesh who is unable to "exercise ungodly dominion over the earth"!

What Do You Have That You Did Not Receive?

As a child I was told by society: "Work and you'll eat." Perhaps you were taught this too. I believed that if I worked hard enough and long enough, I could meet my needs. But as I have grown older, I have seen that hard work is not always the answer to supplying one's needs. I recently saw an elderly gentleman standing on my neighborhood street. He held a sign for the passing traffic to read. In bold red letters it pleaded: "Work Please," and listed his name and telephone number. Surely—I thought as I went about my weekly shopping—this man is not lazy. He truly wants to work. Is he a victim of the present depressed economy? Is he an unskilled laborer, never having been taught a trade? Can he read and write well enough to fill out a job application? Perhaps he had worked hard and long for many years but was recently replaced by a computer or some other technological wonder.

The apostle Paul asked the proud Corinthians: "What do you have that you did not receive?" (I Cor. 4:7). I often ask myself this question. Why should I have plentiful food to eat, a good education, a nice house to live in, and appropriate clothes for my family, while the man holding the sign does not? Do you believe, as I have come to believe, that these things are simply a gift from God? Nothing more. You and I are not more special to God than any of his other children. And while we may use more of its resources, no one owns the earth. "The earth is the LORD's and the fulness thereof," states the psalmist (Ps. 24:1). We simply use it for the little while we are here. The fact that we have enough to eat and a place to live is a treasure from God, not something we deserve. We brought nothing into this world (I Tim. 6:7). It is only by cultural *fortune* that we have what we have. And it is only by cultural *misfortune* that most of the world's inhabitants don't have enough to sustain their lives.

It Is Later Than You Think

Throughout this chapter I have focused on the disadvantages of the world's poor. Let us turn the focus on ourselves for a moment. How do the world's poor affect us in our everyday living? Judging by the standards of most people in the world, we live with abundance and have our needs met sufficiently, if not lavishly. By our life-style, we may be forcing options on the poor around us. Consider the alarming crime rate in this country. I personally know of few people who have not had their homes burglarized and their valuables stolen. Many victims of crime now lock and bolt themselves up in homes that resemble small forts in their efforts to protect their possessions. How many people, both young and old, turn to a life of crime—stealing, pushing drugs, and even murdering others in their attempts to get money? This nation's prisons are full. Those who have possessions have become direct targets of those who do not. It is really much later than we think. Our own survival is now at stake. Our own safety and well-being, both nationally and personally, is being jeopardized.

Perhaps you and I should indeed learn to use our own money more wisely to help those who cannot help themselves. For in doing so, we will not only be feeding and clothing and sheltering families in need, but we may be protecting ourselves and our families as well.

What Can You Do?

I have simply stated the problem of world poverty. Declaring that a problem exists is easy. Finding a solution to that problem is not so easy. As a concerned Christian consumer, what can one do to help solve the problem of global poverty and hunger? Through my research I have found a few suggestions.

You Can Have Compassion

Perhaps you have never been hungry. Perhaps you have never missed a meal. If so, you probably cannot adequately understand the plight of the hungry. While you cannot have empathy, you can have sympathy for the crowds that know hunger hourly.

Jesus had compassion. He struggled with the starving masses. The writer of the Gospel of Matthew (Matt. 15:32–38; cf. Mark 8:1–10) tells us of a certain preaching and healing service Jesus conducted on a mountain near the Sea of Galilee. Jesus had been healing the lame, the crippled, the blind, and all the sick peole who had gathered around him. After several days, he stopped and looked out over the crowd of people who were listening to his words. Jesus must have seen the hunger written on their faces, and the weak and trembling knees when they tried to stand. The Bible tells us that Jesus realized they had had nothing to eat for three whole days. He called his disciples over to him.

"I have compassion on the crowd," he told them. "They are hungry, and I don't want to send them away hungry. They might faint on the way home."

No doubt the disciples gave Jesus a funny look, shrugged their shoulders, and wondered how Jesus was going to feed a multitude when they couldn't even feed themselves. Without acknowledging their lack of faith, Jesus asked: "How many loaves of bread do you have?" "Seven, and a few small fish," they replied. Then Jesus told the crowd to sit down. He took the lunch that was meant for one, thanked God for it, broke it, and told the disciples to pass it out to the hungry crowd. The Bible says they all ate, all four thousand of them, and they were satisfied.

Jesus had compassion on the crowd. He knew what hunger felt like. After all, he had been in the wilderness for forty days without anything to eat. He had felt the emptiness in the pit of his stomach. He had coped with the physical weakness and the throbbing headaches of hunger. He had endured the gnawing, gripping hunger pangs that only bread can relieve. He understood hunger; he had empathy, as we would say.

Only after you and I have endured the pain of hunger ourselves can we feel that kind of compassion. Some Christians I know have decided to fast regularly. They tell me that even one day a week will convince anyone that hunger, even for a short time, can consume you. Few things hold interest for the person who is hungry. You may decide to fast too. If you do, fast for one day. Then imagine not having breakfast to break the fast on the next day. Nor lunch. Nor dinner. Imagine watching your body become thinner and weaker from lack of food. Try to put yourself in the place of a victim of poverty who has no meals to anticipate.

When Jesus felt compassion, he prayed for the hungry, and then he shared what he had with them. Have compassion on the crowd. For compassion often leads to action.

You Can Become Involved

"But I am only one person. What can I possibly do to solve the problem of world hunger and poverty?" This is a question

I ask myself again and again. This is a question I hear others ask as they look in defeat at the problem of the poor.

Again I look to Mother Teresa for an example. An elderly but strongly motivated woman, she has done her small part, on the global scale, in caring for the poor. Perhaps you cannot trek off to India or South America or Africa. Maybe you've got a family, a job, and other responsibilities that would make it impossible for you to lead the life of a Mother Teresa. Still, if you feel compassion and want to get involved, you can do plenty right here at home. "But I'm only *one* person," you insist. Mother Teresa has an answer for you: "We ourselves feel that what we are doing is just a drop in the ocean. But if that drop was not in the ocean, I think the ocean will be less because of that missing drop" (Quoted in *Seeds,* Feb. 1983, p. 4). With this attitude, she has made the difference between death and life for thousands. You can too.

You Can Pray

Pray that God will burden your heart for the poor and hungry. But beware! Prayer leads to action. Praying to God to burden you and direct you is a dangerous request. Only God knows where a prayer like that may lead you. Before Jesus broke the bread to feed the hungry crowd, he prayed. God answered his prayer and made him the vehicle by which thousands were fed. Be ready when God answers your prayer.

You Can Love Your Neighbor

Do you genuinely love your neighbor? It's hard to love someone you have never met. It's easier to love your friends and neighbors and fellow church members in your own community. How can you have genuine love for a starving family in Brazil or an elderly man or woman in the streets of

Calcutta? Perhaps the story Jesus told about the good Samaritan explains genuine love at its best. A badly beaten and half-dead man lay on the road. Two persons, a priest and a Levite, passed him by. The third person, a Samaritan, stopped to help him. He wrapped his wounds and took him to an inn. He also paid for his medical care. He loved him even though he did not know him. He saw a need, felt compassion and genuine love, and gave of himself and his money to help this stranger, his neighbor (Luke 10:29–37).

Do you possess genuine love for the poor, sick, and dying, the kind of love the Samaritan showed for his unknown neighbor?

You Can Learn About World Poverty

Become knowledgeable about the problem of world poverty. Augustine once said: "Love without knowledge goes astray, knowledge without love puffs up, love with knowledge builds up." Learn all you can by reading about the subject. Through information from books, magazines, newspapers, and television, keep abreast of current needs in developing countries. Good books abound on the subject of world poverty and hunger. If you know missionaries in impoverished countries, write to them. Ask them if you can sponsor a family in need of food, clothing, and housing. Inquire how you can best help needy individuals. Through your church or denomination, ask for suggestions about where you can help others in need.

You Can Give Your Money

Maybe you can give only a small portion of your income to the cause of fighting world poverty. But when your money joins the money of thousands of other concerned Christians, you can make a difference in the lives of families in many parts of the world. Your money can go to help support missionaries who work directly with the poor. There are many international, national, and community organizations that help feed the hungry and clothe and house the poor. You can join and contribute to one or more of these. Through your local church or denomination, you can give to special hunger projects. I recently read that church members belonging to the Southern Baptist Convention gave more than $5.8 million for world hunger and relief in 1982. Within the last five years, when Southern Baptists became more aware of the problem, world relief giving increased some 600 percent. (*Seeds,* April 1983, p. 24.)

You Can Give Yourself

No matter how small or how large your efforts, you can make a difference in someone's life. Chances are, when you think of eliminating world poverty, you think of an overwhelming feat to accomplish. But take a moment to look at your next-door neighbor, or your fellow church member, or the elderly lady who lives in the next community. Could some of these people be hurting? Could they be hungry? Could they be going through hard times and need money? Could they be sick and need to hear an encouraging word?

Whenever I think of a person who gives of herself, I think of my grandmother, Alice Crane Williams. Even at eighty and in failing health she carries on her personal ministry. I call it her "telephone ministry." She doesn't drive, so she cannot easily visit the homes of the sick and the poor. But whenever she hears of people in her family, her neighborhood, or her church with a need, she calls them. She checks on them daily, and lets them know she cares. Always searching out the shortages of others, she knows who needs warm blankets in the winter, or clothes for their children. "Mama," as I call her, collects the blankets and clothes, washes and irons them, and sees that someone delivers them. And if anyone lacks food, Mama keeps a storeroom of canned garden fruits and vegetables to give them. No one does without as long as Mama knows of the need. I once remember a little ragged girl selling flimsy, discolored dishcloths who knocked at Mama's door. Mama not only bought the dishcloths but slipped the barefoot child a big handful of change "just for her."

What contribution does Mama make to the battle against world poverty? In her own special way, she ministers as she knows how to those right around her, and she makes a difference in the lives she touches.

I recently read of two more examples of self-giving. One California woman with a family spends most of her time raising money for relief of world hunger. She collects coupons, holds church dinners, and involves everyone she knows in the effort. She also hosts dinners for hungry unemployed persons and their families in her suburban community. In one six-month period, she gave out more than 350 baskets of food to the needy in her neighborhood. While she could use her own family or her twelve-hour-a-day job as genuine excuses for not becoming involved, she doesn't. She gives of herself to the cause of fighting hunger in the world and in her own neighborhood.

Another woman, in Maryland, has turned her four-bedroom suburban home into a shelter for the homeless in her county. She and her husband have fixed up the house for the homeless, and have moved themselves into a small apartment in the basement.

One of my favorite passages in the Bible is Matt. 25:35–40: " 'For I was hungry and you gave me food, I was thirsty and you gave me drink, I was a stranger and you welcomed me, I was naked and you clothed me, I was sick and you visited me,

I was in prison and you came to me.' . . . 'Lord, when did we see thee hungry and feed thee, or thirsty and give thee drink? And when did we see thee a stranger and welcome thee, or naked and clothe thee? And when did we see thee sick or in prison and visit thee?' . . . 'Truly, I say to you, as you did it to one of the least of these my brethren, you did it to me.' "

When you give of yourself to one of the least of those in need, you give of yourself to Christ.

You Can Work Through Your Church

When your efforts are joined by thousands of other Christians who share your views, you can greatly multiply your effect. Here are a few examples of what you can do through your church to help in the battle against poverty.

1. Support your missionaries who work directly with people in underdeveloped countries. Work to meet their needs so that they can better meet the needs of others.

2. Initiate special offerings when money can be collected from church members for world hunger and other worldwide poverty projects.

3. Form a committee within your church to study and learn about the hunger needs around the world and in your own community. Educate your members by sharing current information. Tell them what they can do to help. Get them involved.

4. Organize a clothing and food pantry in your church. Establish it as a permanent part of your church program. Ask your members to donate canned food and good used clothing. Set up a room or storage area, and let the community know you have food and clothing for them when they need it.

5. Start a special "help" fund to raise money for those in your community who cannot pay high utility bills in winter. Form a small committee to search out the needs of your

neighborhood and distribute the money where needed.

6. If you have a basement or large area in your church building, start a hospitality ministry. Provide a warm, safe place for the poor transients of your city to sleep at night. Ask volunteers in your church to coordinate the project and be responsible for its upkeep.

7. Organize a soup kitchen in your kitchen. Perhaps your church has a kitchen and members who will volunteer their time to cook and clean up. Open the doors of your church kitchen as many days as possible and feed the poor and the hungry. The food doesn't have to be fancy. But do make it hot, hearty, and nourishing. If your church cannot finance the kitchen completely, ask merchants in your community to help donate or purchase food.

8. Teach your Sunday school children about world poverty. Let them get involved in projects. In this way, you'll teach them to be concerned Christians and better consumers. You will direct them in their own ministries to have compassion for the underprivileged. Start Sunday school class goals, such as saving canned foods in the classroom closet. Or start a special fund to help provide books or school supplies for children in developing countries. You and your children will make a difference in the lives of people around the world and in your community, and in your own lives as well.

9. As a congregation, write letters expressing your concern. Get together in small groups and write letters to members of Congress asking for policy changes in government programs. Correspond with world hunger groups and ask where you can concentrate your efforts as a church. Write to your missionaries and let them know you remember them and want to help them in their ministries.

10. Get together with other churches in your city. Organize and start new programs with the added strength this

provides. The Old South Church in Boston, a Congregation-al/United Church of Christ church in downtown Boston (where I worked for three years), has recently been involved in a program called "Saturday's Bread." Through this joint project with other Boston churches it cooperates in feeding more than 150 homeless and poor people every Saturday with "friendliness and dignity." A Methodist church supplies the kitchen and dining area, and each congregation pledges financial support and volunteer workers. A volunteer nutri-tionist plans the meals. With the six or eight teams of people who work approximately four hours each, the total number of hours involved for each volunteer in the course of a year is small. Perhaps you can start such a project in your own church and city.

You Can Work Through Your Community

Perhaps you live in a community of people who are also concerned about world poverty. Many of the church projects I have mentioned can also be organized in your community. Pay special attention to the changing needs of your communi-ty. Perhaps you live near a factory that has just been closed. Find out the needs of the newly unemployed workers. Maybe you live in an area that has just experienced a flood or a fire. Investigate the needs of the victims. Participate in community fund-raisers for world hunger relief and community help projects. These might be sponsored by various hunger and poverty groups and may include fund-raising dinners or walks for hunger, or both.

You Can Work Through Your School

If you are a student and your college, university, or seminary does not have an organization on campus to study the problems of world poverty, start one. Select a few concerned people to form a committee. Then invite others to join. Hold seminars and see that others on campus are alerted to the needs. You may want to invite guest speakers from outside the campus, or to enlist faculty, staff, or student speakers from your school. Through literature posted on campus bulletin boards, given out through campus post office boxes, or handed out in the hallways between classes, seek to educate your student body. You can also sponsor fund-raising lunches and walks and other activities to raise money for world poverty projects.

You Can Live More Simply

How you live can greatly influence how others in the world will live. "The rich must live more simply that the poor may simply live," states one writer. (Charles Birch, "Creation, Technology and Human Survival," *The Ecumenical Review,* Jan. 1976, p. 70.) Spend less on expensive food, furniture, cars, and houses, and more on your needy neighbor. Sit down with your family and evaluate your life-style. Could you live more simply? Ask the members of your family to list ways each can help save on the earth's resources. As a Christian consumer, you can do a great deal in your own life-style to help others throughout the world. (For more examples of simple living, read the next chapter.)

You Can Prevent Waste

You and I live in a country that has twenty million dogs, 73 percent of which are overweight! Americans spend enough money on junk food to feed the people of the three largest nations in South America! (Tommy Starkes, quoted in *Sprouts,* March 1983, p. 6.) Every day, you and I witness waste in our federal government. We see money wasted in our supermarkets, with vast amounts spent on packaging and advertising instead of on food. We see money wasted in our churches. We waste money in our own homes. As Christian consumers, it is our responsibility to be good stewards of the earth's resources, using only what we need, sharing with others, and seeing that nothing is wasted.

You Can Become a Peacemaker

How can becoming a peacemaker help the cause of the world's poor? Consider what war does to millions of people throughout the world. It kills innocent people, including fathers and mothers, and leaves starving and unwanted orphans. It demolishes buildings, homes, places of work, whole villages. It contaminates water supplies. It destroys schools and farmland. It creates food shortages. These are only a few of the devastations of war. Rebuilding and starting life again may not be possible for victims of war. If rebuilding is possible at all, much work and many resources will be needed.

"Blessed are the peacemakers," Jesus said. Become a peacemaker! Write letters, alert others to peacemaking, learn about what you can do as a peacemaker, read current peacemaking material, oppose governments that spend vast amounts of money on more and more arms, support programs in your church, community, and nation that promote peacemaking, and pray for peace. In money alone, peacemaking could make a considerable difference. "If the awesome total of about $1.3 billion that the world now spends *daily* on arms were frozen, even at this too-high level, the money to eliminate hunger could easily be found. The cost of a single intercontinental ballistic missile could plant 200 million trees, irrigate 2.5 million acres, feed 50 million malnourished children in developing countries, buy a million tons of fertilizer, erect a million small bio-gas plants, and build

65,000 health centers or 340,000 primary schools." (Indian Prime Minister Indira Gandhi, quoted in *Sprouts,* Nov. 1982, p. 6.)

You Can Learn from the Poor

Have you ever considered that the poor of the world can teach you and me something of great value? Those who are poor, and who have become accustomed to, and settled into, their life-styles, can teach us to be content with what we have. The apostle Paul writes: "I have learned, in whatever state I am, to be content" (Phil. 4:11). Perhaps the poor who are content in their poverty know something about life and about Jesus that you and I don't know. For how many times, even in our abundance, are we discontented with all that we have, and want more?

The poor can teach us about the simple life-style—how to get along with much less than we now have. They can show us what is really needful to our existence.

They can also teach us about how to share with others who are more needy. There are people—perhaps you know some of them—with less money and fewer possessions, perhaps even facing severe hardships, who give much more generously to the poor than you or I do. Perhaps they can show us how to use our own money more wisely and less selfishly.

Conclusion

In closing, let me confess to you that I have only scratched the surface of the problem of world poverty. It is a dilemma that will probably be around for your children, your grandchildren, and even your great-grandchildren to try to solve. But as a Christian, you share a oneness with all of the world's citizens, all of God's children, whom Christ loved and for whom he died. It is hard to be patient while thousands of people worldwide are starving each day. But it is also hard to change the opinions of people and governments overnight. Be patient. Be prayerful. Be prepared to work hard at answering God's call as he directs you in your own personal ministry.

The reasons for world poverty are varied and not easy to understand. But one thing is certain: you and I, as Christians, and as Christian consumers, can make a difference. You can have a direct impact on the whole world or on your next-door neighbor. By being concerned, giving of your money and of yourself, living more simply, wasting nothing, and possessing the love and compassion of Christ for the unnamed multitudes, you can make a difference.

Why should you and I, as Christian consumers, be concerned about the world's impoverished people? Because you and I have abundance, and they have little. Because you and I, and every hungry man, woman, and child, belong to the same kingdom of God. Because you and I, as citizens of a "rich" nation, have the power to make changes. And because Jesus loves the poor and he tells us also to love them.

The hungry people of this world have something to teach us about our own lives.

Allow me to close this chapter as I began it, with Mother Teresa. "The greatest evil," she states, "is the lack of love and charity, the terrible indifference towards one's neighbour who lives at the roadside assaulted by exploitation, corruption, poverty and disease. . . . Only in heaven will we see how much we owe to the poor for helping us to love God better because of them." (Muggeridge, *Something Beautiful for God,* Introduction.)

Chapter 5

Working Toward a Simpler Life-Style

As a Christian, and as a consumer, would you like to simplify your life-style? This chapter contains some reasons *why* you should try to develop less complicated ways of living, as well as some specific ideas about *how* to go about doing so. These suggestions are certainly not all-inclusive. But I hope they will help you to start working toward a simpler life-style.

Why Should You Develop a Simpler Life-Style?

1. You and I should live a simple life because Jesus lived simply. As Christians, we must strive to live the most Christlike life possible. When you focus your life upon Jesus, when you become truly Christ-centered, you won't be attached to the material possessions this society holds so dear. You will live for the glory of God, not for material wealth. Paul said: "Whatever you do, do all to the glory of God. . . . Be imitators of me, as I am of Christ" (I Cor. 10:31; 11:1). Jesus offers you a gift—the gift of simplicity.

2. By simplifying your life-style, you will better appreciate those things that money can't buy—the things in life that are truly important, such as family, friends, good health, and

creative recreation. You will experience a freedom from possessions and status-seeking and the burdens of ownership.

3. You will build more quality friendships. Gone will be the material things that kept hidden your true qualities as a person. Concentrating on people will become more vital to you.

4. With fewer needs, you will have more money to give to those who are in need of life's necessities.

5. You will make a difference in the lives of future generations. As a Christian consumer living in a nation that indulges itself, adopting a simpler life-style will allow you to use less of the world's limited resources. Paul Ehrlich explains: "The average U.S. citizen 'has roughly 50 times the negative impact on the earth's [resources] as the average citizen of India.' The world cannot afford U.S. consumption patterns. Those of us who live in at least relative affluence must cut back toward some kind of *just* standard of living." (Paul Ehrlich; quoted in James B. McGinnis, *Bread and Justice: Toward a New International Economic Order*, p. 326.)

The American Indians lived on this continent for thousands of years in complete cooperation with nature. Many tribes were careful to plant a seedling tree for every tree they uprooted to use. They existed simply, and allowed nature to furnish their daily needs. How very much life-styles have changed in just a few years. We as a nation have mistreated nature, laying heavy demands upon it and, at the same time, stepping on it and destroying its yield!

By simplifying your needs you will use less of the earth's natural resources and thus cause less pollution of the earth, air, and water. And you will leave something valuable and life-sustaining for your children and grandchildren.

6. You will have a stronger Christian witness. Others will notice your life lived in obedience to Jesus' teachings. They

will see that you are truly concerned about the world's needy, with whom you have begun to share more of your time and money. What better example can you set for your children, your family, your friends, and your neighbors than that of following the example of Christ?

7. By caring less about hoarding up treasures for tomorrow, you will be less anxious about your future. Jesus points to the birds of the air and the lilies of the field and tells us not to worry about such things as food or clothing, for "your heavenly Father knows that you need them all" (Matt. 6:32). "Therefore," he continues, "do not be anxious about tomorrow" (Matt. 6:34). And, Jesus teaches us to pray: "Give us this day our *daily* bread," not bread for tomorrow, next week, or next year, but just for today (Matt. 6:11).

Indeed, as you look toward retirement one day in the near or far future, as you see the elderly in this country who count pennies to buy groceries, and as you hear of the nation's social security program becoming more shaky every day, living a simple life-style and trusting Jesus for your future needs will require a rare faith.

What Is Simplicity Anyway?

Vernard Eller describes simplicity as "a lessened evaluation of what the world promotes as important." (Eller, *The Simple Life*, p. 114.) The pursuit of simplicity is somewhat like a race. It is your own personal journey from the ways of this society. To be sure, it should be a quiet race, as to run it proudly or boastfully defeats its purpose.

I will never forget the first Boston Marathon I attended. The runners had one goal in mind: to run the race and to cross the finish line. To reach their goal, they unburdened themselves of all unnecessary equipment. They wore only those clothes needed for modesty. They carried nothing that would weigh them down. Throughout the race, the runners kept a steady pace, never looking back, always looking toward the finish. When they reached the difficult point in the run, a place they named "Heartbreak Hill," they had to make a firm commitment to stay in there and endure the rest of the journey.

Perhaps that is the kind of race Paul refers to when he talks about life in Christ: "Let us also lay aside every weight . . . and let us run with perseverance the race that is set before us, looking to Jesus the pioneer and perfecter of our faith" (Heb. 12:1-2).

How Can You Start to Simplify Your Life-Style?

Developing a simple life-style takes a period of adjustment. It means diminishing your supplies, changing your spending habits, teaching your family about simplicity, and learning to do without the things you have grown accustomed to. But you can start your jouney toward simplicity right away.

In Your Home
When you buy or rent your home, make good use of the space you pay for. Guest rooms, formal living rooms, and other rooms you use infrequently might be an expensive waste for you. Choose a location near your work, schools, and shopping. This will cut down on commuting costs and time.

Furnishings. Furnish your home with furniture that will last. You can find sturdy pieces at moving and yard sales that can be refinished or reupholstered. Plan to keep your furniture until it wears out.

Energy. Learn to conserve. Keep only the appliances you really need. Turn off lights in rooms you are not using. Wash and dry full loads of clothes only, and keep filters clean. Bake in your oven in large quantities. Keep the thermostat as low as possible to conserve heat. Ask your furnace or utility company to give you an energy analysis of your home. Many firms will do this free of charge. Always keep doors and windows closed tightly, and close off any rooms you do not use often. Learn to use less water for bathing and for washing clothes. Repair leaky faucets, as a leak of only one drop per second adds up to 650 gallons per year! Keep your appliances, furnace, air conditioner, etc., maintained and in good repair so they will be as energy efficient as possible.

Christian Community. This might seem like a drastic action to you, but moving into a Christian community does have certain advantages. You will have others to help you keep your commitment to a simple life-style. Your need for possessions will greatly diminish, since you will share everything with others. You will not worry about home ownership and repairs and upkeep alone. Each person will be able to do what he or she does best, thus easing the work load on the individual. You will live in a community of Christians of all ages, and share a treasure of fellowship. Community living among Christians dates back to the early church, and it is making a comeback as Christians today realize the advantages of this simple life-style.

Good Records. Keep good records of your home expenses and your energy costs. This will not only reward you with deductions on your income tax return; it will allow you to evaluate your spending habits on a regular basis. Watch to see if your expense patterns are changing to conform to your simplified life-style.

In Your Personal Needs

A simpler life-style can also be achieved in regard to food, clothing, money, and personal habits.

Food. Simplify your meals. Buy only nutritious food and don't buy snacks, candy, and refined sugar. Cut down on meat. Eat eggs, cheese, yogurt, and milk instead for your animal protein. (Many nutritionists consider the egg the most perfect form of protein. After all, it has all the qualities to sustain the life of a chick!) Take advantage of supermarket specials and money-saving coupons. Buy fruits and vegetables in season. Eat leftovers. Don't buy convenience foods—they are easy to prepare but much more expensive to buy. Learn how to store food properly to prevent waste. Buy and cook in large quantities and freeze for later use. Grow some of your own food and freeze or can the surplus. Join or organize a food cooperative. When you entertain guests, serve simple food and emphasize the people instead of the dinner. Have potluck dinners and ask each guest to bring a dish.

Clothing. Buy only basic and durable clothing. Forget fashion trends and buy clothes and shoes that look good, that fit, and that are comfortable. Select natural fabrics rather than synthetics. Check the labels in clothes when you buy, and make sure they can be easily and inexpensively cared for. Watch for out-of-season sales, and coordinate your purchase with the rest of your wardrobe. Buy clothes that are appropriate for the climate. Take advantage of clothing cooperatives, especially for children's clothes that are quickly outgrown. If you sew, buy fabric on sale and make your own clothes.

Jewelry. Avoid excessive jewelry. You might want to dispense with it altogether, since it can be expensive to buy, expensive to insure, and causes unlimited worry as to its being stolen.

Insurance. I believe in buying good insurance. For some people, this contradicts with their view of a simple life-style. They believe that living simply and trusting Jesus for daily needs is sufficient, and that no one needs insurance coverage. But suppose your home burns and you lose everything you have. What becomes of your life-style then? Will you have to work two jobs to get on your feet? Will you worry and fret over providing the basics for your family? Insurance that covers home and furnishings and medical expenses is necessary. It will enable you to stay debt-free and continue your simple life-style even in the face of tragedy.

Having good insurance has another advantage too. Suppose you cause someone else injury or loss, as in an automobile accident. Is it not your Christian responsibility to give financial aid, to help that person get back on his or her feet without heavy future financial concerns?

Shopping. Learn to buy only what you really need. Change your shopping habits. Don't shop for recreation. Avoid impulse buying. Remember to keep your shopping trips short, lest you be tempted to buy unneeded merchandise.

Personal Habits. Change your personal habits. Do you smoke? Do you munch on junk food between meals? Do you collect items that serve no purpose other than collecting dust? If you have a habit that complicates your life-style, try to change it.

Your Money. Begin to part with your money. Little by little, let loose of the grip on your purse, and give to the needy. It will become easier as money becomes less important to you. You will watch more carefully what you keep for your own real needs.

Personal Care. Take good care of yourself. Sickness interferes with a simple life-style. It takes time to recover from sickness, and it's expensive. Since strength is required to maintain your new life-style, eat well, exercise regularly, relax and renew often, and remember to have regular checkups.

Read and Learn. Other authors have dealt with the simple life-style in much more detail than I have in this chapter. Let me suggest to you several good books that I refer to most often: *The Simple Life,* by Vernard Eller; *Beyond the Rat Race,* by Arthur Gish; *Living More with Less* and *More-with-Less Cookbook,* by Doris Janzen Longacre; and *Lifestyle in the Eighties* and *Living More Simply: Biblical Principles and Practical Models,* edited by Ronald J. Sider.

In Your Family

When changes will affect the members of your family personally, decisions for a simpler life-style should be made together.

Priorities. Determine your own and your family's priorities. Sit down with your family and decide together what you need and what you can live without. Then sell or give things away. Unclutter your life.

Gift-Giving. Reevaluate your gift-giving. I have never understood why almost all holidays include gift-giving as part of their tradition. So often holidays mean crowded department stores, long checkout lines, overextended credit, unwanted gifts, and tired feet. Why couldn't more emphasis be put on family togetherness and celebration? Sit down with your loved ones and talk about gift-giving practices for the future. Decide to give simpler and less expensive gifts, perhaps handmade items, or to stop exchanging gifts. You might want to spend the money instead for food baskets for the needy in your neighborhood. Would that not greatly simplify your life and ease your strained holiday budget?

Your Children. Teach your children to live simply. No doubt peer pressure plays a big part in your children's yearning to buy things. If one child has a certain toy, then another child will probably want one just like it. Sit down with your child and ask the reasons why he or she wants something. Evaluate together what it will cost in time and money if it is purchased. Stress the truly important things in life over the material things, and pray that your children will keep your simplified ways when they establish homes of their own.

Commitment. Ask the members of your family to join you in seeking to maintain a simple life-style. Many temptations will lure you to give up your simplicity. It is important to make a commitment together, as each of you will be a vital link in making it work.

In Your Transportation

Use public transportation whenever possible. If you need a car, buy one that is fuel efficient. Have it maintained regularly. Trade only when it becomes unsafe to drive. When weather, time, and distance allow, walk, bicycle, or jog instead of driving your car. Make a list and combine your shopping errands all in one run.

In Your Job

Take your simple life-style to work with you. Use only the energy you need to get a job done. Take your lunch so as to save money and avoid the noontime lunch rush. Carpool with fellow workers, or take public transportation if it is available, instead of driving alone. If you are responsible for purchasing office or factory equipment, buy energy-efficient machinery and only what you need.

In Your Recreation

Plan simple recreation—biking, hiking, swimming, walking, visiting friends, etc. Map out your long-distance vacations carefully, taking advantage of discount and off-season rates on airlines, trains, buses, and package tours through reputable travel agencies. Try to avoid the commercial hotels. Instead stay with families in bed-and-breakfast homes and hostels, or swap homes with people who want to visit your area for a while. Read travel books about how to save money on places to stay, means of travel, meals, etc.

If you enjoy eating out for recreation, cut discount coupons from newspapers and watch for restaurant specials. Eating out at lunch often provides the same menu for considerably less money. Read about how to eat wisely, nutritiously, and inexpensively. For example, the American Heart Association distributes a pamphlet on creative cuisine, and offers hints on eating out and staying healthy.

Take advantage of free community or church recreation. Watch your newspaper for special exhibits at libraries and museums. Some churches have a gymnasium that families can use, or will rent the local YMCA or YWCA one evening a week for their members. Catch the matinees of movies, plays, etc., and pay less than for evening performances.

However you choose to relax, make sure your recreation fosters your simple life-style. You may want to forgo the big two-week vacation splurge each year, and take short weekend trips instead. Above all, make your recreation safe and fun.

In Your Church

The earliest groups of believers practiced a simple church life-style. They renounced their rights to their possessions. They used what little they had for the benefit of the Lord's people. Money-making schemes, fund-raisers, and new church building programs were not considered by them. In Acts 2:44-45 we are told: "And all who believed were together and had all things in common; and they sold their possessions and goods and distributed them to all, as any had need."

Would you enjoy worshiping with those early Christians? Do you wish you could step back two thousand years and leave behind the large and expensive church buildings of today, with their stage lighting and sound systems, thickly padded pews, and spacious, paved parking lots?

In an essay entitled "The Church as a New Community: Fostering a Simple Life," Gottfried Osei-Mensah describes the real concerns of the church as fourfold: (1) The spiritual health and eternal welfare of our community and its members; (2) our witness concerning God's goodness, justice, and saving power; (3) the investment of our life in God's service; (4) our responsibility to make a difference in the investment of our money and material resources. (Gottfried Osei-Mensah, in Ronald J. Sider, ed., *Lifestyle in the Eighties*, p. 133.)

How can you bring these ideals back into the life of your church? Get involved with the committees that make the decisions about money, building projects, and church planning. Make known your ideas on simplifying the programs in your church with your fellow committee members. Ask that they spend the money on nurturing people and self-help programs instead of extensive building projects. Oppose any misuse of time or money in the church that could better serve a need elsewhere. Share your faith and your discoveries about your own simple life-style with your fellow church members and with the leaders of your church.

In Your Community

Through cooperation with your neighbors and community organizations you can both help yourself and benefit those in need.

Fellowship. Seek fellowship with those in your community who have also made a commitment to the simple life. This will make living the life easier for you. Exchange ideas and ways with each other to further strengthen you and aid in your future simplification.

Borrow and Share. Why do you and your neighbor both need a lawnmower or a set of tools? Simplify your needs and borrow each other's things. Buy needed possessions together, and share the upkeep and repair expenses.

Barter. Instead of paying for goods and services, trade for them. Barter. If you hate to cook, find someone in your community who loves to cook but who has no family to cook for. Then agree to buy the food, and invite the cook to dine with your family in exchange for preparing the meal. Both of you win. The same idea can work with housecleaning, gardening, and baby-sitting. You will exchange only time and work, no money. By bartering, you will be doing more of the things you enjoy, less of the things you don't enjoy, and you'll be saving money too.

Get Involved. Organize and support groups in your community that work to protect your environment and to conserve the earth's natural resources. Your simple life-style will include a sincere concern for others who share this planet. Start drives to recycle paper, cans, and bottles. Alert others as to air pollution and hazardous chemicals dumped into our soil and water supply. Boycott, and encourage others to boycott, the use of dangerous chemicals and products that are harmful to the environment and to unknowing consumers worldwide. Be concerned about the poor in your community, and organize community gardens, food and clothing cooperatives, and other programs to help them. Strive to teach others in your community how to respect nature and treat the earth with kindness, so future community members will be able to also enjoy its harvest.

In Your Earning, Spending, and Investing

When you earn, spend, and invest your money, be careful to do so with Christian integrity. Let others see Christ in you even in your marketplace dealings. Do not compromise your Christian beliefs or your simple life-style as you seek to earn a living for yourself and your family. Spend your money only for those things you need. When you invest your money, make sure your investments are used carefully and honestly and with good Christian results. Invest in people. Investing your money may mean giving your money away to those in need. While you will not receive financial dividends, as with other financial investments, you may receive dividends much more valuable than mere money, as your money will help sustain and change lives.

Conclusion

What can you expect from working toward a simpler life-style? You can expect better health, for you will be walking, biking, and relaxing more often. You will worry less about overwhelming bills and overextended credit because your needs will be simpler. More quality time to spend with your family and friends will be a result of your new life-style, since you will be free from time-consuming possessions. You will make an important worldwide contribution as you learn to use fewer of the earth's resources and share more of what you have with others in need. You will set a better example for your children and teach them to follow in your footsteps. You will have fewer anxieties about your future since you'll be taking one day at a time and trusting in God for your basic needs. And your Christian witness will be stronger as you follow the example that Jesus set for others to see.

Developing a simple life-style won't be easy. It won't happen overnight. You'll need time to learn to live simply, since you and I have been conditioned by society that "bigger and more is better." It will take a special calling and commitment to stick with it—a commitment that will need daily renewal by you and your family. It will take planning and hard work to learn to depend less on material things. It will require unlimited contentment not to yearn for what others have. And it will take courage to live a simple life, since you must hear criticism from unsympathetic people who won't understand your motives.

You and I have now come to the end of this chapter and to the end of this book. Our journey together has been brief. Much has not been said.

My prayers go with you as you run your race in this life. May you unburden yourself of all those things that would weigh you down. May you keep a steady pace, never looking back, always looking toward the finish. And when you encounter hard times in your trip, may you "stay in there"! With God's help, the rest of your journey will be easier because *you* are traveling lighter!

Questions for Thought and Discussion

1. Have you ever been, or are you now, a victim of excessive spending, of unbridled consumerism? How did you, or how can you, correct the problem?

2. What do you believe Jesus' words to the rich young ruler in Luke 18 meant? How do they speak to you and me today?

3. As a Christian consumer, how can you strive to put money in its proper place? What do you consider the proper place for money?

4. Do you believe that advertising can be an unfair and deceptive means of selling products?

5. How can you guard yourself from the deceptive hypnotist—advertising?

6. Why do you buy the things you buy?

7. Do you consider your possessions your master or your servant?

8. How can you resist the temptation to impress your neighbor with material possessions, to keep up with the Joneses?

9. Do you have more material possessions than you need or want? Would you like to do something about it? What can you do about it?

10. As a Christian, are you concerned with the problems of world hunger, disease, and widespread poverty? What do you consider your responsibility to others in need in the light of Jesus' words?

11. Are you satisfied with the way your church spends money? If so, why? If not, how could your church better invest its funds?

12. What is your definition of a "simple life-style"?

13. Would you like to live a less complicated life-style? In what ways can you start to simplify your life?

14. How can you become a more knowledgeable and responsible Christian consumer? In what ways can you teach your children to become responsible consumers of the future?

15. How do you feel becoming a more concerned Christian consumer can help your Christian witness? What could it say to those around you?

Bibliography

Alexander, John F. "Does Money Matter?" *The Other Side*, Nov. 1981, pp. 40–43.

Allen, Susan. *Your Money's Worth*. Danbury Press, 1974.

Bailard, Thomas E.; Biehl, David L.; Kaiser, Ronald W. *Personal Money Management*. 3d ed. Science Research Associates, 1979.

Barnette, Henlee H. *The Church and the Ecological Crisis*. Wm. B. Eerdmans Publishing Co., 1972.

Birch, Charles. "Creation, Technology and Human Survival," *The Ecumenical Review*, Jan. 1976, p. 70.

Boerma, Conrad. *The Rich, The Poor—and the Bible*. Westminster Press, 1978.

Bornkamm, Günther. *Jesus of Nazareth*. Harper & Brothers, 1960.

Brady, Edward J. "What Does the Lord Require?" *Seeds*, April 1983, pp. 7–11.

Braidfoot, Larry. "Strengthening Families and the Economic Crisis," *Light* (Christian Life Commission of the Southern Baptist Convention), Jan.-Feb. 1983, pp. 11–12.

Byrd, H. Davis. "World Hunger and American Christians," *Religion in Life*, Spring 1980, pp. 49–64.

Cailliet, Greg; Setzer, Paulette; and Love, Milton. *Everyman's Guide to Ecological Living.* Macmillan Co., 1971.

Chandler, Bea and Dave. "Saving for Tomorrow?" *The Other Side,* Nov. 1981, pp. 14–17.

Donnelly, Doris. "The Needle's Eye: Christians and Their Money," *The Christian Century,* April 27, 1983, pp. 400–402.

Dowling, Michael J. *Health Care and the Church.* United Church Press, 1977.

Eller, Vernard. *The Simple Life.* Wm. B. Eerdmans Publishing Co., 1973.

Faw, Bill. "Our Daily Bread," *Sojourners,* Jan. 1980, pp. 22–24.

Fleming, Daniel Johnson. *Ventures in Simpler Living.* International Missionary Council, 1933.

Galbraith, John Kenneth. *The Affluent Society.* Houghton Mifflin Co., 1958.

Gentry, Kenneth L. "Book Report," *Fundamentalist Journal,* March 1983, pp. 37–39.

Gish, Arthur G. *Beyond the Rat Race.* Herald Press, 1981.

Graham, Fred W. "America's Other Religion," *The Christian Century,* March 17, 1982, pp. 306–308.

Grant, James P. "The Children's Revolution," *Seeds,* Feb. 1983, pp. 7–11.

Greinacher, Norbert, and Müller, Alois, eds. *The Poor and the Church.* Seabury Press, 1978.

Hengel, Martin. *Property and Riches in the Early Church.* Fortress Press, 1974.

Hinds, Michael deCourcy. "Consumer News," *The Courier-Journal* (Louisville, Ky.), Feb. 27, 1983, p. H10.

John Paul II, Pope. "The Poor Will Eat and Will Have Their Fill," *L'Osservatore Romano,* N. 31 (745), Aug. 1982, pp. 1,

2, 8. Homily delivered Sunday morning, July 25, 1982, during Mass at Castel Gandolfo.

Johnson, Luke T. *Sharing Possessions: Mandate and Symbol of Faith.* Fortress Press, 1981.

Kilgore, James E. *Dollars & Sense.* Abingdon Press, 1982.

Lappe, Frances Moore. *Diet for a Small Planet.* Ballantine Books, 1971.

———, and Collins, Joseph. *Food First: Beyond the Myth of Scarcity.* Houghton Mifflin Co., 1977.

Leclercq, Jacques. *Christianity and Money.* Hawthorn Books, 1959.

Longacre, Doris Janzen. *Living More with Less.* Herald Press, 1980.

———, *More-with-Less Cookbook.* Herald Press, 1976.

Ludwig, Thomas E., and Myers, David G. "How Christians Can Cope with Inflation: Getting Off the 'Hedonic Treadmill,' " *The Christian Century,* May 30, 1979, pp. 609–613.

McCormack, Arthur. *World Poverty and the Christian.* Hawthorn Books, 1963.

———, ed. *Christian Responsibility and World Poverty.* Newman Press, 1963

McGinnis, James B. *Bread and Justice: Toward a New International Economic Order.* Paulist Press, 1979.

McKeever, Jim. *The Almighty and the Dollar.* Omega Publications, 1981.

Martin, Hugh. *Christ and Money.* George H. Doran Co., n.d.

Maupassant, Guy de. *The Complete Short Stories of Guy de Maupassant.* Doubleday & Co., Hanover House Book, 1955.

Muggeridge, Malcolm. *Something Beautiful for God: Mother Teresa of Calcutta.* Ballantine Books, 1973.

Niebanck, Richard J. *Economic Justice: An Evangelical Perspec-*

tive. Division for Mission in North America, Lutheran Church in America, 1980.

Niebuhr, H. Richard. *The Responsible Self.* Harper & Row, 1963.

Packard, Vance. *The Hidden Persuaders.* Pocket Books, 1957. (Rev. ed., 1981.)

———. *The Status Seekers.* David McKay Co., 1959.

Prior, K. F. W. *God and Mammon.* Westminster Press, 1965.

Quint, Barbara Gilder. "Breaking Up Is Expensive to Do," *U.S. Air,* Oct. 1982, pp. 25–28.

Rasmussen, Larry L. *Economic Anxiety & Christian Faith.* Augsburg Publishing House, 1981.

Reader's Digest Association. *How to Live on Your Income.* Reader's Digest Association, 1970.

Reich, Charles A. *The Greening of America.* Random House, 1970.

Schumacher, E. F. *A Guide for the Perplexed.* Harper & Row, 1977.

———. *Small Is Beautiful.* Harper & Row, 1973.

Schweitzer, Albert. *Reverence for Life.* Pilgrim Press, 1969.

Short, Mark, Jr. *The Bible and Business.* Broadman Press, 1978.

Sider, Ronald J. *Rich Christians in an Age of Hunger.* Inter-Varsity Press, 1977.

———, ed. *Cry Justice! The Bible on Hunger and Poverty.* Paulist Press, 1980.

———, ed. *Lifestyle in the Eighties.* Westminster Press, 1982.

———, ed. *Living More Simply: Biblical Principles and Practical Models.* Inter-Varsity Press, 1980.

Stamp, Sir Josiah. *Christianity and Economics.* Macmillan Co., 1939.

Tapp, Robey. "Women, Infants, and Children," *Seeds,* Feb. 1983, pp. 12–13.

Toffler, Alvin. *Future Shock*. Random House, 1970.

Ward, Barbara. *The Rich Nations and the Poor Nations*. W. W. Norton & Co., 1962.

Zablocki, Benjamin David. *The Joyful Community*. Penguin Books, 1971.

Notes